Financial Survival for Oil & Gas Workers

Tips for coping with a volatile industry

Peter Wang, MS PG MBA CRPC®

ISBN: 1523806842
ISBN-13: 978-1523806843

DEDICATION

To the Memory of

Tieh Chun Wang, MD (1926 – 2015)

CONTENTS

PREFACE BY THE AUTHOR

On Thursday, March 19, 2015, at about 10:00 AM, I got laid-off from my job with a leading oilfield services company, after a fourteen year career. My N+2 manager asked me to come to "a company meeting", where I met with a nervous group of managers. I experienced the classic combat stress reactions; tunnel vision, black spots, rapid pulse, shallow breathing, and auditory exclusion (muffled sounds heard as if from a distance); as the manager started talking about "the unprecedented decline in oil prices... forcing a major revision of our business plans... we're sorry, Peter, today is your last day..."

It was all so humiliating. It was really difficult, as the primary breadwinner male, to face my wife when she came home that day. I broke down and wept on her shoulder. It was the worst day of my life up until that point. Fitting that it should happen during Lent: "....though I walk through the Valley of the Shadow of Death..." When my daughter heard the news, she went off to a room in her high school and cried. Her application for a college scholarship through my former employer's charitable foundation was automatically canceled the moment I was terminated, along with our family's health and disability insurance.

More than nineteen months have passed since that dark day. I have been one of the extremely fortunate ones, as I have been working almost continuously in my field since, at decent wages to boot, with only one month idle. My daughter is thriving at college. My wife is at peace. Despite my good fortune, I believe the layoff will remain in my life as a bright, traumatic line of demarcation. Time will always be divided into "before 3/19/15" and "after 3/19/15". And the danger has certainly not ended. Oil is still only $50 per barrel. Anything could happen.

People who experience a trauma typically re-live the experience in their minds. They ruminate and ponder what has just happened to them, in order to make sense of it all, to extract some meaning from the experience. I have been no different in this regard. I have found myself facing several questions:

- Why did the layoff happen?
- Did I miss any advance warnings of the layoff?
- Could I have better prepared for it in any way?
- Was it a bad idea to have pursued an Oil & Gas career to begin with? I decided to become a Geophysicist in 1979 at age eighteen; what advice would my old self give to my young self?

As time has passed post-3/19/15, I have realized I do indeed have some of the answers to these and other difficult questions. Influenced by our education, our family upbringing, our own natural tendencies, and luck, my wife and I managed to put into place over the years a web of practices which have served to keep our family safe since 3/19/15, and should continue to function into the future. I would like to tell you how we did it.

This book emphasizes making preparations. I don't discuss much what to do after a layoff. Once you are laid-off, it is the depth and quality of your prior prep that will greatly govern your post-layoff experience. Once you are laid-off, your economic boundary conditions are set in stone, and you simply have to ride it out. I would rather devote these pages to getting you as well-prepared as possible for any adverse event, and hopefully, no adverse event at all.

Most importantly, I have managed to answer the final question, "Should I have pursued this career at all?". In order to make the question practical and forward-looking instead of introspective and backwards-looking, the question should be restated as, "Should young people consider an Oil & Gas career?" I believe the answer is a qualified "Yes". "Yes, young people could consider an Oil & Gas career, if it appeals strongly to them, if they can bear the risks… and because the risks are significant, extra precautions are warranted". My recommendations for precautions are described in this book, with separate chapters for all stages of life and career.

I am honored to dedicate this book to the young people who wish to pursue a career in Oil & Gas, despite the poor publicity the field is receiving since the oil industry Depression started in late 2014. Consider the information on these pages to be much a part of your personal and family protective gear as your hardhat, hand and eye protection, steel-toed boots, and fire-resistant coveralls.

Houston, Texas, October 2016

1 OIL PRICES

Oil prices - the wellspring of blessing and curses

It does not take long for any Oil & Gas worker to realize that the industry lives and dies based on the price of oil, and therefore oilfield employment, hiring, and firing swings wildly with oil prices as well. Exactly how wildly can be seen if we search the Internet for some data.

In this chapter, we are going to take a look at:

1. How severe these price swings have been over time
2. Why they occur
3. Are there simple "career early warning systems"?

A century and a half of instability

If we search the Internet using search terms "oil price" we will find many charts that show the highly volatile price of oil over the years. In order to make a fair comparison between today's oil price and oil prices from many years ago, we must use the "real" or inflation-adjusted prices, since we know that a US Dollar from the past buys more than a US Dollar today. Prices not adjusted for inflation, in the US Dollar "of the day" are called "nominal" prices. The oil company BP publishes an informative chart of oil prices, at BP.com > Energy economics > Statistical review > Oil > Oil prices. This chart, reproduced in Figure 1, shows year 1861 - 2015 oil prices in nominal US Dollars, and also oil prices in 2015 real (inflation adjusted) US Dollars in Figure 1:

Oil prices

Dated Brent averaged $52.39 per barrel in 2015, a decline of $46.56 per barrel from the 2014 level and the lowest annual average since 2004

Crude oil prices recorded the largest decline on record in dollar terms, and the largest percentage decline since 1986. The annual average price for Brent, declined by 47% reflecting a growing imbalance between global production and consumption. The Brent-WTI differential narrowed for a third consecutive year, to $3.68 per barrel.

Crude oil prices ($ per barrel | world events)

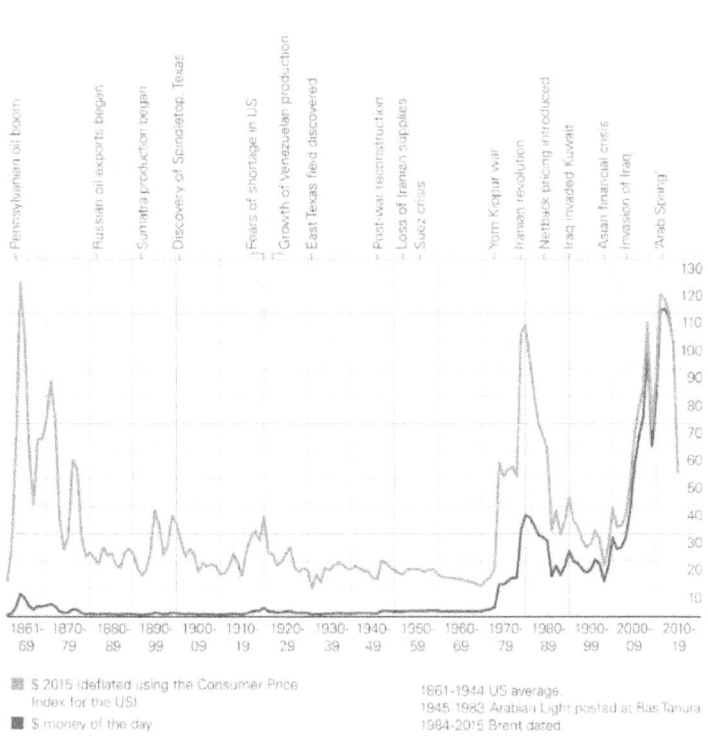

Figure 1 - Nominal and real oil prices (BP)

What Figure 1 shows is that the real oil price, the price we care about (the light green line, in 2015 US Dollars per barrel) were very high during the the US Civil War years, then they were volatile but trending downward until about 1880. From 1880-1973 they were on a long-term trend downward, with some volatility, and amazingly, this cheapening of oil in real terms was not even significantly impacted by the turmoil of two World Wars! But suddenly, after the 1973 event known to US consumers as the Arab Oil Embargo, the 2015 Dollar real oil price surged almost *ten-fold* from about $10 to over $100. This reversed, and by 1986, the prices were about $30. Prices crashed further by late 1999 to under $20. Then they reversed, and by mid-2008, just before the Great Recession, they were over $110. The chart ends showing the latest steep price crash into the low $50 range by the end the chart. As we all know, the story evolved further into 2016.

Figure 2 below, a chart of West Texas Intermediate Crude (WTI) prices from the US Energy Information Agency, helps us to fill in the time period since mid-2015, which the BP chart does not show. This is a much more detailed chart, showing daily prices for WTI crude oil. Because there hasn't been hardly any inflation from 2014 to 2016, it's permissible to consider nominal and real prices as being the same. We observe that by July 2014, WTI prices started a steep decline, plunging to $26.19 on February 11, 2016. As of the day of this writing (October 2016), the price is about $50.

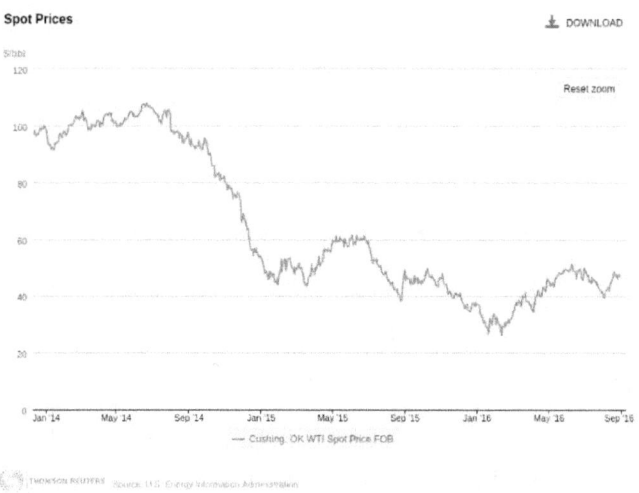

Figure 2 - Nominal West Texas Intermediate Crude prices (US EIA)

We see in the historical record a century and a half of oil price instability, since the very dawn of the oil era, continuing on into the present day. And closer to the times in which we live, over the 43 year old lifespan of a middle-aged person, since 1973, oil prices in real terms went up 10x, then decreased by 5x, then increased by 5x, then decreased by 4x. Sudden price declines like the most recent 2014-2016 decline, cause huge problems for employers. Their budgets quickly are made irrelevant. In the business lingo, they have "no visibility" into their profit and loss position. They find it difficult or impossible to hang on to employees, or even to keep operating at all, depending their financial condition.

Lynxes and Hares

So why are oil prices so volatile? While it is impossible to predict the price of oil from day-to-day, it is possible to understand some of the drivers that force oil prices up and down. These become clearer with the benefit of hindsight. As we know, "hindsight is always 20/20". Interestingly enough, there are analogies to oil and other commodity prices and natural systems. Let's consider Lynxes and Hares.

The Lynx, a predatory cat, hunts and eats Hares, a vegetarian prey animal. If the Lynxes, as a group, happen to have a lot of success in hunting, they will become well-fed and healthy, they will hook-up with other Lynxes, and there will be Lynx pups - more mouths to feed. Eventually, the Lynx population will grow to the point where the Hares get over-hunted, and their population will decline, and possibly crash if there is a hard winter or other adverse event. If their numbers decline swiftly, the Lynxes will simply starve. If enough Lynxes starve and die, then the Hares will be able to stage a comeback with fewer predators coming after them. And so the cycle repeats. Each end-state of the system… high Lynx population, or high Hare population… is inherently unsustainable, and the system inevitably oscillates.

It's a similar situation in the oil business. A favorable oil price and the potential for good profits draws investors into the oilpatch. But as more players enter the market, more oil gets produced. As we know from basic economics, if a market becomes oversupplied with goods and services, the price offered by consumers declines. The price can stay up so long as supply and demand are in balance, but if more oil comes on-line than can be used by the world's consumers, the price will inevitably fall.

A parallel development occurs in oilfield services. The oilfield services companies follow the Exploration & Production (E&P) companies in, and if their services are somewhat scarce and in high demand at the time, they will be able to demand high prices from their customers and make good profits themselves. These profits draw investors in, and new firms will be formed to serve the market. As oilfield services becomes oversupplied, prices there too will fall, because of competition, and if oil prices are also retreating, the E&P companies profits fall, or they start taking losses. At this point, they cannot justify spending as much on oilfield services as they did before; they put the squeeze on their suppliers, or the orders simply slow and stop.

Under some market conditions, the largest producers - Texas USA for most of the 20th Century, and then Saudi Arabia after 1973 - can act as "swing" producers, moderating and stabilizing market prices by modulating their production. But, in doing so, they give up market share, and leave money on the table. So once in awhile, the swing producers simply get tired of that role, and they will try to punish the other market participants, by strongly ramping up their own production, and letting prices crash in hope that weaker players will be forced out of business. We are in such a phase now. During Thanksgiving 2014, OPEC, led by Saudi Arabia, decided they were tired of being the world's swing producer, and they decided to not give up any more market share to North American shale producers. Oil prices crashed precipitously at the close of that meeting.

You'd think in an oil price decline rational companies would just shut-in production and wait it out. The problem is oil is a heavily financed industry. The terms of loans to E&P companies demand payment, no matter what - the imperative for companies is to keep the oil and cash flowing and keep as many of the loans current as possible, even if they are producing the oil at a loss.

After many quarters of financial losses, previously enthusiastic investors will begin to act in a risk-averse manner towards making further Oil & Gas investments. As the lines of credit disappear, the ability for companies to pay for further drilling, completion, logging, seismic, software, and pumping decreases. Remember, Oil & Gas reservoirs naturally deplete, and companies have to pour in money to keep running in place on the production treadmill. Eventually, the ability to keep producing large physical volumes of oil will decrease.

On the demand side, consumer enjoy the lower oil prices. Sales of large gas-guzzling trucks and SUVs generally expands during oil prices crashes. Cheap oil undercuts alternative energy investments, and currently, cheap natural gas is even displacing coal as an energy source. It is thought that the natural gas industry is more to blame for the coal industry's woes than Greenpeace.

Eventually, as demand rises, and as production declines because of too few new investments, too few workers, and because of old, wrecked, and cannibalized equipment, Oil & Gas become relatively more scarce, and prices increase again. And the cycle repeats, like the Lynxes and the Hares.

Early Warning Systems

It is in this seemingly endlessly chaotic environment that all of us enter school, graduate, begin our Oil & Gas careers, and then eventually, we end our careers... either voluntarily or involuntarily. We can do absolutely nothing about the accident of the timing of our life. And we can do absolutely nothing about the price of oil, and relatively few of us can influence how well the industry or our employer is equipped to deal with these prices.

Does that mean we can do nothing to manage how oil price fluctuations affect us and our families? I do not believe that. I think we can gain some insights from industry data, and get some advance warning, enough time to get ready for a possible personal financial earthquake.

The U.S. Geological Survey has set in place earthquake and tsunami warning systems that give the operators of critical infrastructure components like nuclear power plants, subways trains, and airports a precious few seconds and minutes to insert control rods into nuclear reactors, stop the trains, and keep planes from landing in case of an earthquake. Should they ever be utilized, the warnings given will never be far enough in advance, because of the high velocity of earthquake waves; but they will be better than no warning.

I propose that we in the industry all make use of the commodity and financial information available for free around-the-clock on the Internet. Not only is raw data available, but there are many clever financial charting and analysis tools available for free as well.

Now, it is impossible to cover a complex topic like technical chart analysis even if I were to devote this entire book to it, and I am by no means a Certified Market Technician (CMT), but I can demonstrate a few basic principles and suggest how you might use them.

For those of you with no familiarity with financial jargon, data, or charts, please do not be intimidated. I suggest you just bravely dive in and follow me step-by-step on your computer as I describe the procedures for making some charts which will be useful in keeping watch over possible storms brewing in your Oil & Gas career.

Please follow step-by-step

First of all, let's look at a basic chart of WTI crude oil prices from StockCharts in Figure 3. You just navigate to www.stockcharts.com on the Internet, and type in "$WTIC" in the "Enter Symbol or Company Name" box, then hit the "Go" button. The type of chart you want to make is just the default type, a "SharpChart". To exactly duplicate what I did below, I changed the Period from "Daily" to "Weekly", and I only kept one Overlay, a "Simple Moving Average" with a period of "40", the other overlay I set to "-None-", and I set the Range to "2 years" (don't type any of the quotation marks I have used into StockCharts; they are just to make things clear for you. Quotation marks will confuse Stockcharts).

Figure 3 - Weekly price chart of $WTIC, West Texas Intermediate Crude

The blue, smoothed line is what is called the "40 week moving average of West Texas Intermediate crude". Because there are five trading days in a week, the 40 week moving average is about the same as the 200 day moving average. Both will give similar results.

How do you compute the 40 week moving average of West Texas Intermediate crude? Stockcharts just takes the price of WTI crude oil at the close of business on Friday afternoon for the last 40 weeks, mathematically averages them together, and posts that average on the most recent Friday on the chart.

Moving averages are useful to analysts because they show long-term underlying trends in prices without the day-to-day "jitter" or "chatter". What is really useful about moving averages is when you get a "moving average cross", where a price crosses over its own moving average. This can often indicate a change in the long-term trend, the beginning of one of the many "bear" (prices decreasing) or "bull" (prices increasing) market which are seen in Figures 1, 2 and 3.

Referring back to Figure 3, the price of WTI crude, shown in red, white and black "candlesticks", was diving below and popping above the 40 week moving average line frequently since the end of the Great Recession, from 2010 onwards. But notice what happened to the blue line around August 1, 2014. The candlestick price bars dived underneath the 40 week moving average line and they kept on going down. This is a classic long-term "bear market" technical indicator. This is a warning sign of further price weakness.

This moving average cross took place shortly before a very steep, deep price decline. In retrospect, because hindsight is always 20/20, we can see that something quite bad was shaping up by October 2014. The moving average cross took place almost four months before the fateful Thanksgiving 2014 OPEC meeting, and almost eight months before I was personally laid-off; and I was one of the earliest layoffs in this cycle. I wasn't paying attention to the WTI price action in 2014, but I really should have been. I would've had many extra months of prep time. As it was, I was not expecting to be laid off; I was caught very much off-guard.

Is $WTIC the only ticket symbol to look at? By no means. For those interested in natural gas, if you work for a natural gas company, the symbol to use is "$NATGAS".

You can also get Oil & Gas prices from the U.S. Energy Information Agency. The web address is www.eia.gov/dnav/pet/pet_pri_spt_s1_d.htm

Figure 4 - Energy Select SPDR Fund, ticker symbol XLE

Figure 4 shows the symbol "XLE", which represents an exchange-traded fund (ETF) which contains the stocks of a basket of large Oil & Gas firms, so this price is a proxy for Oil & Gas industry health. Notice the 40-week moving average cross took place in September for this fund; more than a month later than for $WTIC. In other words, Oil & Gas investors didn't figure out what the change in oil price really meant until a month after it started declining, but when they did, they starting dumping Oil & Gas stocks.

When investors think a company (or group of companies, like an ETF) has a good chance of making a profit, they buy the stock, and the stock price gets bid up. If they think it will be a money-loser, they sell the stock, and the stock price declines.

Why might you want to monitor Oil & Gas company stocks using XLE instead of the hydrocarbon price directly? Well, for one thing, no one actually is "employed by the price of oil". People work for companies, which are all part of an industry. By watching oil industry health, you are getting closer to what you care about, which is... *"are they healthy enough to keep paying me?"*

Figure 5 - SPDR S&P Oil & Gas Equipment and Services ETF, ticker symbol XES

Figure 5, symbol XES, which represents an ETF of oilfield services companies, has showed a much steeper loss of value since the 2014 peak, reflecting the fact that oilfield services firms have suffered earlier and worse than their customers who are reflected by XLE. The moving average cross took place in late July 2014. If you work for an oilfield services company, you should monitor this ETF. This is the one I look at.

One problem with ETFs is they haven't been around for a long time. Their older cousins are called Mutual Funds. If you look at energy industry Mutual Funds, you get a longer-term glimpse into the history of Oil & Gas industry health; and written into those charts are the untold stories of people getting hired and people getting fired.

The Fidelity Select Energy (FSENX) and Energy Services (FSESX) mutual funds are similar in coverage to XLE and XES, but they have a longer history, going back to 1981 and 1985. These long histories are quite interesting to look at, see FSENX in Figure 6 below which shows 1990-2016:

Figure 6 - Fidelity Select Energy Mutual Fund, ticker symbol FSENX, 1990-2016

Oil field veterans will remember the layoffs on this chart that most companies went through: early '90, late '90s, early 2000s, 2009, and currently 2015-2016. The 40-week moving average cross precedes all of them.

If you work for a publicly traded company, you can, of course, follow your own company stock using Stockcharts.com. If you work in precious metals mining, try "GDX". If you work for base metals mining, try "DBB". GDX and DBB are ETFs for those two mining sectors.

Is the moving average cross an infallible indicator? No, the price being tracked periodically dives below and surges above the 40-week moving averaging, a process called "whipsawing", where a price cross is suddenly reversed a few months later. Does this mean it's a useless indicator? Of course not; isn't it better to respond to a danger sign which turns out to be a false alarm and a fire drill, than to be walking around in the dark and suddenly fall into a hole without any warning? Personally speaking, I would have done things differently if I'd been tracking the price more diligently in late 2014.

In order to preserve your sanity, I would suggest not being tightly plugged into the 24-hour business news cycle. At most, check oil prices and stock prices once a week. More often does not help. For example, there are two well-known tactical asset allocation investment strategies, one by Gary Antonacci and the other by Dr. Mebane Faber, which use momentum indicators and moving averages, and both their trading systems specifically recommend to "Look at your investments once a month and forget about them the rest of the time." In other words, they encourage you to live your life. Checking and making decisions more frequently does not add value. In fact, looking less frequently is by itself a whipsaw filter. Sound advice. I wish I could always follow it.

If we get crosses below the 40-week moving average in the future, does that mean we should panic and run to the hills? I would say no, never panic, but it means you should definitely start positioning yourself for something worse that might be coming down the road.

Most of what I describe in the rest of this book are long-term preparations that will hopefully be put in place before the storm hits, and truthfully, they take a long time to put in place no matter what the price of oil is doing. Learning how to budget and control the Dollars in your household takes time and effort. Building up a large Oil & Gas industry sized emergency fund takes time, probably years. Paying off your mortgage takes time. Planning your alt.career takes time. So no matter what the oil price is doing this day, isn't it a good idea to start getting your life in order so that in the end you'll be able to take whatever life and this volatile industry dish out?

2 BUDGETING

The financial survival techniques outlined in this book are based on a couple of simple facts:

1. Oil & Gas jobs pay very well, when the industry is not in recession or depression
2. When the industry is in recession or depression, you may lose that job

Therefore, you must underspend your salary during good times, so you save a large emergency fund for bad times. How large an emergency fund should be is the subject of Chapter 4, and that's a question that does not have an easy, one-size-fits-all answer.

If, during the good times, you consistently spend all of your salary and have insufficient savings, or worse, if you consistently overspend and carry a debt load, you're not in a good position to withstand the loss of your salary. In order to underspend your salary, you and your spouse or domestic partner need to have and adhere to a monthly budget that prioritizes saving for industry downturns.

I can't overemphasize the importance of household budgeting, debt elimination, and savings. When I was laid-off in 2015, our family had zero debt and a very large amount of savings, and I was still an emotional wreck every day until I found work. I imagine the additional stress of too-little savings combined with debts must push some people over the edge. Indeed, we are seeing the toll on individuals and families starkly reflected in the headlines:

CBC News Calgary, December 7, 2015 - Suicide rate in Alberta climbs 30% in wake of mass oilpatch layoffs

Every incremental suicide, broken or abusive marriage, or grieving soul driven to alcohol or drugs caused by industry downturns is unacceptable and tragic. But since employers often do little or nothing to help their former employers, and because government aid to the unemployed in the USA is quite thin, we have to learn how to help ourselves.

Fortunately, there are self-help resources. I am pleased to recommend that you look up the great work in the field of household budgeting, debt elimination, and savings that has been done by Dave Ramsey. I believe in building on top of the good work of others, and not trying to re-invent the wheel. Dave's website is at www.daveramsey.com, and his content is available for free or at low cost via that website, books, radio broadcasts, podcasts, YouTube, and in Financial Peace University, a training course taught by volunteers, mostly at churches throughout the United States and Canada.

Dave teaches that families should strive to accomplish several "Baby Steps" on their way to financial and mental peace. The language below is taken directly from his website:

"The 7 Baby Steps

Step 1: Save $1,000

$1,000 to Start an Emergency Fund - An emergency fund is for those unexpected events in life you can't plan for. Whether there's a plumbing issue and everything but the kitchen sink is draining, or your brakes are squealing at every stop sign, you can be ready!

Step 2: Pay Off Debt

Pay Off All Debt but the House - List all debts but the house in order. The smallest balance should be your number one priority. Don't worry about interest rates unless two debts have similar payoffs. If that's the case, then list the higher interest rate debt first.

Step 3: 3-6 Month Fund

3 to 6 Months of Expenses in Savings - This step is all about building a full emergency fund. It's time to kick debt for good, with 3–6 months' worth of emergency savings. Sit down and calculate how

much you need to live on for 3–6 months (for most that's between $10,000–15,000) and start saving to protect yourself against life's bigger surprises like the loss of a job. You'll never be in debt again— no matter what comes your way.

Step 4: Invest 15%

Invest 15% of Household Income Into Retirement - Now it's time to get serious about retirement. With no payments and a full emergency fund, put 15% toward the retirement of your dreams. Between your 401(k), Roth IRA, and Traditional IRA, you have a lot of options. Find the fit that is right for you. The money you were using to attack debt can now help build your future.

Step 5: College

College Funding for Children - College tuitions and housing expenses continue to rise. Don't let college sneak up on you. Saving now will put you ahead of the game when your kids graduate from high school. Two smart ways to save for your kids' college are a 529 college savings fund or an ESA (education savings account). These are both tax-advantaged savings vehicles that let you save money for your kids' education expenses.

Step 6: Pay Off Home

Pay Off Home Early - It takes the average family five to seven years to pay their home off early. Just imagine life with no mortgage. There's only one more debt standing in the way of freedom from all debt!

Apply all the extra money toward paying off your home. Not only are you paying off your home early, you'll be saving tens of thousands of dollars in interest fees.

Step 7: Give

Build Wealth and Give - This is the last step and by far the most fun. It's time to live and give like no one else! Build wealth, become insanely generous, and leave an inheritance for future generations. You know what people with no debt and no payments can do? Anything they want! Now that's leaving a legacy."

I mostly agree with this Baby Step list; it's impossible to argue with proven success. However, I do add my own tweaks and criticisms to Steps 3 and 5:

A 3-6 month emergency fund may not be enough for your family. Every family is different, but unemployment in Oil & Gas can unfortunately be very long. See Chapter 4.

Ramsey often states that one's retirement should be, and I paraphrase, "invested in good growth mutual funds, which will return 12% annually". He has repeatedly made statements to that effect on his radio show; I have heard him myself on AM 700 KSEV radio while driving around Houston. But financial experts mostly agree that returns from stocks over the next decade will be low, due to chronically stagnant global economic growth. Optimistically, we're looking at less than half of Dave's 12%, maybe in the range of 5%.

Jack Bogle founded the Vanguard Group, the pioneering American investment management company that manages approximately $3.6 trillion in assets. On October 3, 2016, he was intervied by Christine Benz, Director of Personal Finance at Morningstar. Mr. Bogle predicted:

> 3% returns before inflation, taxes, and fees, for balanced stock and bond portfolio over the next decade

In other words, it would be highly incorrect and dangerous to plan around a 12% return. You'd be guaranteeing to not hit your retirement goals that way. Then you'd become disappointed and give up, which we don't want you to do.

Also, retirement savings should not be automatically equated with 401(k), IRA, and other tax-advantaged types of accounts. The tax advantages are great, but you pay a price. These accounts make it hard to get to your money in the event of an emergency. In my opinion, there is nothing wrong with having some of your retirement savings in taxable brokerage accounts, doing double-duty as retirement and as "deep back-up" emergency fund, meaning, what you spend after your big generous regular emergency fund is gone. And if you never use your deep back-up fund, there are ways to use taxable accounts as part of your retirement strategy so that the tax bite is lessened. We will discuss more ideas along these lines later in Chapter 7.

529 college savings fund and ESAs (Education Savings Accounts) commit money to education that might be needed for survival. These are good types of accounts for tax avoidance, but be careful not to over-save into them, because they will limit your flexibility in times of crisis, just like oversaving into 401(k)s and IRAs for retirement will limit your flexibility, as mentioned above. Am I suggesting you raid your child's college fund to pay the rent? Sort-of. Maybe! Before you condemn me, read about my daughter's

inspiring response to our family crisis in Chapter 6.

Some Ugly Surprises to Budget For

Most people who work in the Oil & Gas industry get a generous benefits package while employed, which completely vanishes when they are unemployed. Therefore, <u>your unemployment budget is going to be different from your employment budget</u>.

Health insurance - you have to buy your own health insurance, either through COBRA (for a limited time only), Healthcare.gov, a health insurance agent, through your spouse / partner employment, or through another group (SPE, AAPG, SEG, AAPL, a labor union, etc.)

Life insurance - you have to have your own life insurance policy to take care of those who depend on you. Ideally, you should have been doing this all along, and not have been depending on your employer's group life insurance. Like Clark Howard and Dave Ramsey, I believe the life insurance coverage for most people should consist of low-cost term life insurance. There is a time and a place for cash value life insurance for some individuals, but when you are unemployed and struggling to make ends meet is not the time nor the place.

Disability insurance - most Americans are inadequately covered for disability when they are employed; when they are unemployed, they are really wide open for disaster. Now, most disability issuers will not write a disability policy for the unemployed; they require a recent and continuing history of earnings before they will insure those earnings; but I found an agent, Doug Roufa, listed in my Appendix B, who will write a policy to high-skill, high-value professionals and consultants. It's worth considering.

An increase in your taxes

Let's say you were to get laid-off late in the calendar year, so you received most of your annual salary. Then you get paid a large severance benefit before December 31. Any unused vacations will also get paid out to you in cash. So now your taxable income for the year in which you got laid-off is huge, since you owe taxes on salary, severance, and vacations. Just when you need it least, the government is going to step in and take 25%, 28%, or whatever your marginal tax rate is multiplied by those payments.

Moreover, if you owe a big chunk of taxes by tax filing day, April 15, and you did not withhold enough the prior calendar year, you will have to pay penalties! So after you are laid off, after you get your severance, you have to estimate your next Federal income tax bill, and make sure you have sent in all of the money you think you will owe to the Feds. This may mean sending in a big check to the IRS as a quarterly estimated tax payment. That's what I had to do. My former employer did withhold from my severance, but not quite enough. I sent in extra payments throughout the year, and by the time tax season rolled around, I didn't own the government anything, in fact, I did receive a refund.

The second effect is this - you also owe more taxes if you start working as a self-employed person after your company job ends. Your employer paid half of your Social Security and Medicare taxes while you were employed; as an independent, you have to pay both sides of the tax, the employer and the employee halves. That would be a total of 15.3% based on 2016 taxes rates.

Truly, it's outrages like these - the severe cost of basic life, health, and disability insurance coverage, and then Federal taxes which are the insult added to the injury of having been recently laid-off - that are driving the disenchantment and anger that many feel towards our political and economic systems and leaders in 2016. These sentiments have driven voters toward insurgent, non-establishment candidates on both sides of the political spectrum and on both sides of the Atlantic Ocean ("Brexit") during this current election cycle. How this will play out through American society in the coming years, only time will tell.

Next Steps

Your next assignment is to put this book down temporarily, and go study the Baby Steps with Dave Ramsey, by Internet, book, or in-person at a Financial Peace University class. After you are through, please come back and read the remaining chapters here. You will learn many more tips and tweaks that will help you adapt Dave's basics to your life as an Oil & Gas worker.

3 EMERGENCY FUNDS FOR OIL & GAS WORKERS

Welcome back to the book. Hopefully you've gone off and done some significant studying and you've figured out how much money you require per month to run your household.

You have returned to this book in order to learn how to right-size your emergency fund based on the fact that you work in the Oil & Gas industry. Dave Ramsey and others often refer to a "three to six month emergency fund".

In Oil & Gas, a three to six month emergency fund might be OK, or it might be way too small. The correct answer is "it depends". It depends on many factors.

What drives how big your Oil & Gas Emergency Fund should be?

- Your monthly household spend
- Do you have a wage-earning spouse or partner?
- How much does you spouse or partner make?
- In the event of an Oil & Gas downturn, what is the risk of your spouse or partner losing their job?
- How soon can you expect to get back to work? Optimistically and pessimistically?
- Are you getting a monthly pension from a former employer(s)?
- When you get back to some kind of work, how much will be making?
- How much severance and unemployment insurance did you get, after taxes?

Your monthly household spend

How much does it take to run your household and take care of everyone's basic human needs on a sustainable basis, where spending is crunched down to the minimum, to the "rice and beans" level, as Dave Ramsey says? You should have gotten that number out of your prior Chapter 2 budgeting exercise and study. For our household, I found out it's roughly $6,000 per month. Everyone will have a different number.

Do you have a wage-earning spouse or partner?

If you do have a wage-earning spouse or partner, how much is their take-home pay per month after all mandatory deductions are taken out of the paycheck?

But it may be unrealistic to assume that they are going continue working, if they are in the same industry sector as you. I know of a married couple, both professionals in Oil & Gas, who both got laid off from their jobs in 2015, they were both on H1-B visas, they had a new baby and a new house, and I suppose they had to go back to their home country. What a heartbreaking story.

If your partner's job is also at severe risk of vanishing, then I would not even consider much of it as available to run the household. Put a 0% or a low probability next to those Dollars. Certainly less than 50%.

How soon can you expect to get back to work?

This is really the toughest question. Although the downcycle which started in July 2014 is not over, and will not be over for a long time, I only suffered one month of downtime, though I did have to change employers twice; the employer I went to during Summer 2015 collapsed due to the oil slump. I know a very few people like me who suffered minimal downtime as well. We were exceptionally fortunate.

The vast majority, however, have been out of work for an extended period - 12 months, even two years, as of the time of this writing (October 2016).

This is obviously not a "V"-shaped industry recovery. It is an "L"-shaped recovery. Realistically, many of the lost jobs will not come back for years, if ever..

Within the context of this recovery, it is unfortunately likely that many of the unemployed will never work in Oil & Gas again, either by choice or unwillingly. That has happened in every major downturn that I have watched; 1986, 1999, 2009, and now 2014. Some people just can't make it back in on the up-cycle. Some of the chairs have been removed from the game of musical chairs.

Because of the severity of the current downturn, I am playing it very cautiously. I am assuming that if I get shaken out of Oil & Gas before the upturn comes:

- I will never work in Oil & Gas again

I am basing all of my plans on that assumption. Yes, it's very pessimistic. Better to plan for the worst, and be pleasantly surprised by the best.

Are you getting a monthly pension from a former employer(s)?

If so, remember to subtract taxes from it. Use your highest or marginal tax rates, not your average tax rates.

When you get back to some kind of work, how much will be making?

If I do leave Oil & Gas involuntarily before the next upturn, my salary expectation will be severely depressed initially relative to my Oil & Gas pay. I am thinking I could get knocked back by -75% during the first year of transition. But I also believe that after five years into my imagined new line of business, I could be making satisfactory pay. Enough pay, at least.

So my emergency fund, and yours too, needs to fill in the missing earnings from the time of layoff to the time when we can thankfully declare the State of Emergency over. And the size of the basket of missing earnings will vary for everyone. That's why a simple rule like a "three to six month emergency fund" is overly simplistic. One size does not fit all.

In the upcoming Chapter 4 for Students, I discuss in detail how students should develop plans for their "alt.career"; I discuss how colleagues over the years have left the industry and have gone on to different fields. I strongly believe everyone in Oil & Gas should have alternative career pathways. So please, continue reading this book, even if you are not a student, or you don't have a child who is a student.

How much severance and unemployment insurance did you get, after taxes?

Don't forget to figure out how much severance you will be getting, and subtract taxes from it. Use your highest or marginal tax rates, not your average tax rates. Also find out from your State Employment Agency how much in unemployment benefits you can expect from them, paid out over what length of time, and then remove what you will pay in taxes in the same manner.

Oh my gosh, this is so confusing, how to I put it all together?

- If you are not retiring, you need to do the spreadsheet exercise described in detail below
- If you are thinking about retiring, you need to skip ahead and read Chapter Seven. If you subsequently decide not to retire after completing the planning exercises in that Chapter, come back here and continue with this spreadsheet exercise

You need to put together a gigantic spreadsheet. Did I mention I love Google Sheets? There will be sixty rows in the spreadsheet, representing sixty future months. Yes, let's take a peek into the next five years of your household economic life. Let's run your household budget better than the Federal Government is run.

The columns will be:

A) Spouse take-home pay, monthly

B) % availability of spouse take-home pay (due to job risk)

C) Severance lump benefit, after-tax

D) Unemployment insurance amount, monthly, after-tax

E) Pension amount, monthly, after-tax

F) What you think your take-home pay could be for each month

G) Your monthly household spend

H) Monthly budget surplus (deficit)

I) Running sum of monthly budget surpluses and deficits

The math is simple, it's:

$$H = (A * B) + C + D + E + F - G$$

And, column I is just the sum of all column Hs. It's a running sum of all of your monthly budget surpluses and deficits.

The two major points are:

On the last row, five years from now, the number in column I must be greater than zero. What this says is… whatever the exact complex pattern for your budget surpluses and deficits, **over the long run, say five years, the household cannot spend more money than it brings in. Period. Full stop.**

The next major point is your Oil & Gas Emergency fund needs to be positive (obviously) and larger than the most negative number in column I. So if Column I, Row 60 is negative $25,000, your Oil & Gas Emergency Fund needs to be positive $25,000. The month during which your cumulative deficit is the worst, is when your family will be experiencing maximum financial stress. If you run down your Oil & Gas Emergency fund to zero at any time during your long transition period, then it's GAME OVER. Well, not over, but things will start breaking severely. So, this fund has to be realistically large enough to buffer the shocks of transitioning to a new way of life.

Now, your Oil & Gas Emergency fund, based on the worst number you see in Column I of your spreadsheet, is only an unemployment emergency fund. It is not designed to cover wrecked cars, leaking roofs, exploding hot water heaters, dead air conditioners, medical emergencies, replacement of stolen or busted iPhones, etc.

Therefore, the TOTAL EMERGENCY FUND = (Oil & Gas Emergency fund) + (Dave Ramsey three to six month emergency fund)

<u>I am guessing if you do the math completely, it could be a very large number.</u> Unfortunately, that is what it takes to survive as a family working in this industry.

Speaking in raw economic terms, Oil & Gas people get paid so much because it's an economically risky profession. People leave or don't enter during withering downturns, and then salaries get bid up on every upturn because over and over and over again since the early 1970s companies have had to steal employees from each other, and entice people from outside the industry to join and move to Texas, Oklahoma, Louisiana, North Dakota, and all of the various garden spots in the Third World.

So what we Oil & Gas people should be doing is saving a huge chunk of our earnings, putting them into our Oil & Gas Emergency funds, and then we should be content to live at a lower standard of living; then we'd be safer in case of an industry melt-down such as we are living through now.

Places to keep your money

I favor the new generation of online-only banks. Our family uses Ally Bank. Other names to investigate are EverBank, Bank5 Connect, Discover Bank, Bank of Internet USA, FNBO Direct, State Farm Bank, Synchrony Bank,

First Internet Bank, and Nationwide Bank. I believe it's important to keep most, if not all, of your emergency fund in a plain old bank, FDIC insured, so that if you need the money, it's there immediately and you don't have to worry about cashing in an investment at a loss, or worse yet, worrying if you're even capable of redeeming an illiquid investment:

NY Times, July 7, 2016 - Growing Unease as British Mutual Funds Block the Exit Doors

A CD is less liquid than a regular savings account. You get a higher interest rate, but if you redeem the certificate early, you face penalties. It could be a good idea to create a CD ladder for your emergency fund, based on the idea that you're not going to have to "eat" your emergency fund all at once the day you get laid-off. You could have some money in a savings account, then in 6, 12, 18, 24,... month CDs. You'll have a CD maturing every 6 months, then you could turn that money around and buy a new CD with it.

Some people favor Credit Unions, based on a buy local, non-profit, anti-bank philosophy, but I generally haven't seen very good rates from credit unions lately compared to online banks.

Our family has taxable brokerage accounts with Charles Schwab. This offers us the ability to shop for the best FDIC-insured bank CDs in a wide variety of maturities and from a wide variety of banks. It's an ideal, convenient "one stop shop" for CDs. We find we can match the online banks in this manner.

You can buy U.S. Treasury bills and bonds directly from the U.S. Treasury Department by setting up an account at TreasuryDirect.gov. These are backed by the full faith and credit of the U.S. Government. They are guaranteed to pay; they don't need insurance. You can buy them in maturities from 90 days to 30 years. And that brings up the next very important point... interest rate risk.

Places to not keep your money

Even a bond which is 100% safe from a default point of view, like a U.S. Treasury, carries interest rate risk. Many people don't know that if interest rates rise, the market value of your bond instantly goes down. So if you buy a long-term bond for $10,000, and you suddenly need it but interest rates went up sharply all of sudden for whatever reason, it's possible you might only be able to get $9,000 by selling the bond on the open market, and that's not an exaggeration. Ouch, this is not the desired behavior for an emergency fund.

Just to clarify some of the terminology used in the bond world, ten-years or longer is considered long-term. Five years is intermediate-term. 90 days - two years is short term. And there are no hard and fast rules, as these are more marketing terms than anything else.

So bonds or bond funds are OK for the emergency fund, so long as they are short-term bond funds. Our family holds these short-term bond exchange-traded funds (ETFs) in our Charles Schwab accounts:

SCHO - Schwab Short-Term Bond ETF (Federally taxable)
SHM - SPDR® Nuveen Barclays Short Term Municipal Bond ETF (the interest is Federal tax-free, but not the capital gains)

But generally, why bother with short-term bonds if Internet banks are paying more? Why not just pile everything into the Internet banks?

The following types of investments are not appropriate for emergency funds - stocks, REITs, long-term bonds, precious metals (physical or ETF), foreign currencies (FOREX), and commodities, futures contracts, inverse (bear market) or leveraged investments. They have their place in your portfolio (maybe), but definitely not as investments that might have to be cashed in next week to pay the rent. They're just all too volatile. You don't need that kind of volatility in your emergency fund.

Dave Ramsey has a humorous observation about how the sexes approach risk. He observes that most women want safe places to keep their emergency money, but some men get impatient with money sitting there making a low rate of interest, then they pursue wildly risky, hare-brained, and inappropriate investments for emergency fund money. He says that "men have no risk bone". How funny.

So we've discussed bank or credit union accounts, Treasury Direct, taxable brokerage accounts, and there is one more type of account you could use for your emergency account, and you may not have heard of it before used as an emergency fund - you could use a Roth IRA.

Should I use a retirement account as an emergency fund container?

Many people do not realize that you can take your original contributions out of a Roth IRA (but not a Roth 401(k)) at any time without tax or penalty. After all, you already paid taxes on your contributions. The restriction is, you cannot take out any growth in the account above and beyond your original contributions. If you do that, before age 59-½ and before the account has been open for five years (the "Roth five year rule"), you do face tax and penalty.

As you get closer and closer to age 59-½, the magic age when you can easily make IRA and other retirement account withdrawals, the required size of your taxable emergency fund diminishes, it only needs to be large enough for your household to "limp" past the age 59-½ threshold. There is certainly nothing wrong with keeping a large taxable emergency fund, though. Money in the bank feels good!

But did you know that anyone can make penalty-free withdrawals from a regular (non-Roth) IRA before age 59-½? I'll bet you didn't know. Here are a few more ways in which you can use a Traditional IRA as part of your emergency fund, or for extra-early retirement:

- Permanent disability of the IRA owner
- Medical expenses in excess of 10% (7.5% if account owner or spouse is 65 or over)
- Medical insurance premium while unemployed
- A series of substantially equal periodic payments. For these payments to be exempt from the 10% penalty, they must continue for at least five years; or until the participant reaches age 59-½, whichever is later; and the distribution amount may not be altered during this period

The computation of "a series of substantially equal periodic payments" requires confusing financial computations, and if you mess it up, you've got the IRS on your tail, which you do not want. You should consult with a qualified tax professional before you try to start pulling out of your IRA accounts before age 59-½.

4 STUDENTS

Perhaps you are a student, preparing for an entry into an Oil & Gas career. You could be in high school, college, or graduate school. Or, maybe you are the parent of such a student. In any case, the remarks on the following pages apply to you.

We have right before us, unfortunately, the case of students who entered university programs in Petroleum Engineering, Geology, and Geophysics in Fall 2012 and graduated in Spring 2016. They were in school when the shale boom was really booming, summer internships were easy for them to get, and there was a lot of talk and promises about how bright their future was, and how the sky was the limit.

Then, in July 2014, after their Sophomore year of college, the price of oil started to dive, and it kept on diving. By graduation in Spring 2016, most of them were unable to find work in the industry. Some who had offers from on-campus college recruiting had those offers rescinded.

This is exactly what happened to my cohort of Oil & Gas workers, those who decided in college around 1979-1980 that the sky was the limit for us in Oil & Gas, but then by the time we emerged with graduate degrees in the mid-1980s, the party was substantially over, and the party-goers were waking up in the gutters with hangovers and soiled clothing. I was one of four lucky new-hire Geophysicists hired by Amoco Production Company's Houston "SETEC" division office in 1986 (Amoco was purchased by BP in 1998). I am certain I called my Amoco recruiter, Dr. Wayne Campbell, a Virginia Tech "Hokie" who has long since retired to Hokie-land, every week prior to my start date to find out if I still had a job.

Then, two weeks after I started working at Amoco, coming to work every day with a briefcase, wearing wingtips, a pin-striped 1980s power suit, and a paisley tie, Amoco had its first mass-layoff ever in its 97-year history (it was

founded in 1889 in Whiting, Indiana), and it was a bad one, something like a 10% cut. And that was one of the first of many that would continue until the final cataclysmic lay-off of most of the remaining Amoco staff more than twelve years later in January 1999, after the purchase by BP was finalized.

So I would say we've gone "Back to the future". The times of 1986 are repeating, thirty years later, as far as the Oil & Gas outlook for students is concerned (left - a promotional poster from the 1985 movie of the same name).

So what then is a student to do?

I think what times like these demand is that you develop "Plan B" skills and capabilities all the way through your educational experience. Yes, this is an additional burden, which will cost you time, money, and energy. But need to do this in case you approach graduation day and you are unsuccessful in landing that Oil & Gas job. Or maybe you land it, but through no fault of your own, you can't keep it.

It makes sense to pursue training and certifications that are recognized by and transferable to other industries. Welders, machinists, pipefitters, electricians, fire-fighters, and commercial truck drivers can work directly in other industries. As you get into more specifically oilfield jobs, it will be harder to convince a non-oil employer what exactly your years as a roustabout or roughneck mean in terms of what you can do for them. The problem is similar to that of former military trying to re-enter the civilian workforce. The military is very specialized, with its own sometimes secretive job categories and lingo. The civilian employer generally doesn't appreciate all that military people do, so they go under-appreciated, and therefore under-hired.

For university students, again, it makes sense to pursue degrees that are recognized by and transferable to other industries. Mechanical, electrical, chemical, and civil engineers can work in various industries. It's tougher for Oil & Gas specialized degree-holders like petroleum engineers and geoscientists.

If you are going to be an Oil & Gas specialized degree-holder, you could pursue an academic minor or certification in something else, something you could also get excited about. And I think here the sky really is the limit; you could make a close-angle pivot and get certified in something very close to your major. For example, a petroleum engineer or geophysicist might minor in math, or computer science. A petroleum geologist might minor in hydrology. Any geoscientist could become skilled in geographical information systems (GIS).

Alternatively, you could make a wide-angle pivot and collect a skill or credential in something entirely different, for example, you could earn a teaching certificate, or minor in business, or if your family has a family business that you never really considered joining (which is perhaps why you went to college), you could invest some time helping in that venture. There is no rule that says a college student can't also pick up a skilled trade, like welding or machining. In fact, such skills could compliment an engineering degree, because then you'd know something about how things really have to get done in the field, and not just how they should get done "theoretically". Field people always complain that engineers send them off to do impossible tasks.

All of these remarks apply even if you have no plans to ever go on to college. Please don't just transition from high school to the drilling rig and then assume you won't ever have to learn anything new ever again. At some point in your lifetime, and sooner than you think, an oil bear market will hit and you will be looking for work, and there will be no jobs to be found in the industry. If you have training and certification that means something to an employer in another industry, in another city or town away from the oilpatch, you will be ahead of the game. If you don't, you may be working minimum wage jobs, even if you made $100,000 a year on the rig.

My own personal story has been that of a wide-angle pivot; I have been preparing to enter the financial services industry in case I get permanently ejected from Oil & Gas. In 1988, after two years at Amoco Production Company, I took the hint from the repeated layoffs and earned an MBA degree part-time at night at the University of Houston. I finished in 1992. Amoco paid my tuition and books; all I had to do was put in the time. Fast-forward to 2016, my wife and I are now empty-nesters, but under the threat of continuing hard times in the oilpatch, I refreshed my 1988-1992 business education by earning the Chartered Retirement Planning Counselor^{SM} (CRPC®) designation online from the College for Financial Planning in Centennial, Colorado. All of these qualifications I am quietly holding in reserve in case I ever need them, because today I am still working full-time in Oil & Gas. But even if I don't use these qualifications, they still literally enrich my life. I use the knowledge to help out my family and my friends.

What is instructive to me is that of our cohort of mid-1980s Amoco Houston geophysicists, wearing shoulder pads and coiffed with "big hair", the vast majority aren't even in geophysics any longer. They moved on to downstream oil refining / petrochemicals, to business consulting, to information technology, and even to the California wine business. Most of them were voluntary leaves... after years of repeated downsizings in upstream Oil & Gas, many of them simply had enough, and decided to pursue other passions.

I am certain on their respective Amoco hire dates, they did not think, "Yes, and in ten years I will no longer be in this company or even this industry". And yet, that is exactly what happened. That seems sad in a way, it seems wasteful to earn a degree in a field and then not use it, but the good side of the story is that it also demonstrates that a good science, engineering, and math education prepares you for many things, and that people are resilient, and are capable of making decisions and working in order to secure their own happiness and security for their families.

My suggestion to all of you who are starting out in Oil & Gas is that you embrace the uncertainty, prepare professionally and emotionally for a couple of divergent outcomes, and then whatever happens, you won't feel paralyzed and without any options.

Student debt, the risk-multiplier

For the first time in history, the amount of student loan debt has recently surpassed credit card debt in the United States. Herein lies a lesson from the often counter-intuitive world of economics. Of course, the expansion of student loans was meant to help students afford college, but it is one of the factors that has made college unaffordable. Let's say you were a butcher, and a customer was coming to your shop with $100 in their pocket, and you knew it, because you had x-ray vision. How much would you try to get from them in the pending meat sale? As much of that $100 as possible, right? Or maybe $100 today, and they can owe you $5, for a total sale of $105?

Well, colleges and universities have x-ray vision that can see the money in your pocket. It's called FAFSA. Even if you personally don't fill out the

FAFSA, they know in the aggregate how much money students come to the table with, both in parent and student savings and in student loans. And like the butcher with x-ray vision, they try to take all of those available funds by raising prices to the unreasonable point they are at today.

You need to resist the urge to take on student loan debt if you are pursuing an Oil & Gas career. Why? Because debt, as any finance student can tell you, is a multiplier or risk and return. Let's say the stock market is giving you a 10% annual return, if you double-up and buy twice as many shares using borrowed money (buying shares "on margin"), you could theoretically make almost a 20% annual return (20% annual return minus the loan interest payment).

But if the market turns against you, and your shares have losses, the debt magnifies the losses. If you sell your shares, you more than have twice the losses, because you had twice as many shares, and you owe interest on the margin loan. So, debt makes downside risk worse.

I am certain there are many who went into debt to study Petroleum Engineering, and as of right now, October 2016, they have no Petroleum Engineering job, and they have student loan payments. Student loans are the worst kind of loans. They are not dischargeable by a personal bankruptcy process. They will literally follow you to your grave, they will even garnish your Social Security check when you are old. Even after death, student loans can get turned over to private debt collectors who will harass and cajole the grieving survivors to pay off their child's or spouse's student loan. This is illegal - but since when did debt collectors ever care about the law?

If you are specializing in an Oil & Gas field, and attending an expensive private or out-of state university through the use of debt, please transfer as quickly as possible to a more affordable public university where you can pay in-state tuition and possibly avoid accumulating more debt. So much the better if you can live at home and attend university.

If you haven't entered college yet, but you're planning to use debt - please don't. Do the first two years in a community college setting while living with your parents, then transfer and finish up the last two years of your program at a state university. If you are still early in high school, you can work very hard and try to get an academic or athletic scholarship to a school where you can pursue your studies. My children earned a significant portion of their college costs through scholarships; this made Dad very happy, and helped the family out tremendously.

Does the prospect of living at home during college sound really unattractive? Does it sound like the exact opposite of the independence you seek as a young person?

Consider this. Student loan debt drags your future lifestyle experiences into the present. So maybe you can seemingly "afford" to live on campus or in your own apartment if you use student debt. But then, the debt burden could keep you from having your future experiences in your actual future, where they belong. This is called **BAD ECONOMIC TIME TRAVEL**. You could be sent back to your parents' home for years after graduation if your gamble does not pay off and you do not find that high-paying Oil & Gas job.

This is precisely what is happening to thousands of new college graduates all across the country, not just those who want to go into Oil & Gas. The percentage of young people in their 20s and 30s living with their parents is the highest it has been since the Great Depression of the 1930s. New household formation is at very low-levels. Marriage and child-bearing are being delayed. The impact on American society of all of this student loan debt is turning out to be profound.

Some sociologists and economists even talk about the "Japanification" of America. Increasingly, in Japan, young people are not dating, not having sex, not getting married and not starting families, and Japanese society is getting older and older. The economy is slowly winding down, particularly becauses Japan is not a country which welcomes youthful immigrant populations. Japan is getting into a trap of perpetual no-growth. That's really bad. Japan's debt-to-GDP ratio is very high, which is crimping their economic growth; future consumption is dragged into the present by economic debt, but then it can't take place in the future, and the future does arrive, someday. America's debt is not as high as Japan's, but it is swiftly increasing. So do the patriotic thing, and just say no to that student loan!

By avoiding debt, you may need extra years to earn your degree. Did you know that most first-time marathon runners do not run; they do a combination of walking and running? You similarly might not be able to just go to classes for four years continuously and get your degree. You may have to have periods of studying alternating with periods of working at a job, or you may need to work throughout, and take a lighter course load. Whatever you have to do to avoid student debt, as long as it's legal and acceptable within your moral framework, do it.

But after you get your degree without the use of debt, you'll be a free man or a free woman. Every Dollar you earn, net of taxes, will be yours to spend or invest as you see fit. A student loan servicing company will not be harassing you even if you have no job upon graduation or a low-paying job.

And if you do manage to land that high-paying Oil & Gas job, and start your working life with no student loan debt? You will be awesome.

5 FRESH OUT, 20S, NO KIDS

The decade of your 20s, just after you complete your formal education, is very important, because during this period you set in stone the work and financial habits that will determine how it all works out for you later in life.

Indeed, during every stage of life, you are planting the seeds of success (or failure) for the next stage in life.

Whether you have landed that ideal, high-paying oil industry job or not, if you have gone through the budgeting exercise of Chapter 2, which can be summarized as "Dave Ramsey's Baby Steps", you will know what I am going to suggest.

Emergency Fund

As discussed in Chapter 3, you need to have a customized emergency fund built to fit your circumstances. In your 20s, before you are partnered and before you have children, it may be a comparatively lightweight emergency fund, compared to someone older who has many life obligations, but don't assume you don't need one. Constructing this fund should be a priority during your first few years of working. You will be able to do this more easily if you employ the money-saving strategies which follow immediately.

Credit Cards

Credit cards and you should be strangers, unless you are the kind of person who can pay the entire bill off at the end of each month. A minority of people can do this successfully. If you can't, then it's not a good idea to get a credit card. If you want one in order to build a credit history, then only use it for paying routine, non-discretionary bills you have to pay anyway; utilities, gasoline, Internet, medical, groceries, insurance. Do not carry it with you. Freeze it in a chunk of ice in your freezer at home. For discretionary purchases, pay with cash or check.

Vehicles

Dave Ramsey says if you have cars and trucks whose value exceeds ½ your annual salary, you have too much car. I agree. Starting out, try to pay cash for the MAV - "minimally acceptable vehicle", otherwise known as a beater. If there was one thing I wish I had done earlier in life, it would have been to be a buyer of used cars. As it was, I saw the light at age 48, and I will probably buy used cars for the rest of my life.

As you gain wealth, you can stop driving beaters, and pay cash for two or three year old used cars with 30,000 - 50,000 miles on them, where the original owner has gotten soaked on the initial depreciation.

Jacked-up, tricked-out trucks? Boat? Porsche? In your 20s? Just say no. Wait until you can pay with cash. Lydia DePillis writes in the October 9th, 2016 Houston Chronicle about an oil worker who:

> "Bought an F-250 with fancy rims - a signal, like being part of a club. 'People are like, "Man, this is a nice big diesel truck, four doors, lifted, nice, man. How can you afford it?" Work in Oil & Gas, he would tell admirers.

This man then was laid-off, and after working in a frozen food processing plant, he finally landed a decent job, but at less than 40% of his prior pay. The news story doesn't give details about the man's finances, nor whether the truck was paid for with cash or debt financed, but the point of the story is that you waste precious resources that could be put to better use than trying to impress people you don't know and maybe you wouldn't like them anyway if you knew them. Should you spend $60,000 on a new truck instead of $12,500 on a gently-used new car (which I did in 2015; and it's a very nice car), the difference being $47,500. As we know, $47,500 will more than feed you for a year. You can't eat your truck.

People who work for the oil industry are mostly allergic to transportation alternatives like carpooling, vanpooling, transit, walking, and bicycling. This is not a helpful attitude. Fortunately for you, if you are in your 20s, you are part of the Millennial Generation, which is *supposedly* not innately suspicious of shared rides and alternative modes, as older generations are. If you can take alternative modes to work each day, you can look forward to saving a ton of money. You will find savings in the area of reduced depreciation on your car (less wear and tear), downtown parking, tolls, and gasoline, in that order. These will be partly offset by the cost of the alternate modes, except biking and walking are almost free. Being car-free is very rough in oil towns like Houston, especially outside of the public transit footprint, but it is possible you could shift from being a two car family to a one car family, with in-fill transportation provided by Uber, ZipCar, and public transit if you live in the transit footprint. Devoted motorcycle riders might successfully avoid having to buy a rainy-day car if they can access transit, carpools, or vanpools during foul weather.

Transit is rarely faster than driving, but even if it takes longer, you can multi-task safely and have an empty personal email inbox and you can be totally caught up on social media by the time you get home. Doing that in your car is a dangerous idea.

The little things add up

Brown-bag your lunch from home. Don't go out to restaurants often for lunch; of course you need to for networking and team-building, but that's not most of the time. If you go out once every two weeks with co-workers, they won't feel like you're abandoning them, you won't feel deprived, and you'll reduce what your lunchtime restaurant bill would otherwise be by 90%.

Don't stop at Starbucks for your morning drink. Drink what they serve at work for free, or if you can't stand it, bring your own ground coffee from home, and a drip filter cone or coffee press. Assuming 235 work days per year, $4 per day savings, a 40 year career, and a modest 5% market return, and your Starbucks is costing you $940 per year, or $113,552 by the end of your career. Is it really worth it?

Construct a work wardrobe that minimizes the need for professional dry-cleaning services.

You can have an attractive watch for a few hundred dollars. The Rolex can wait. Maybe if you're lucky you'll get one from your employer on your 20th work anniversary.

Cable or satellite TV is very expensive compared to cable alternatives like Netflix. I have never managed to justify spending on a conventional cable package. I have also been amazed to discover there are people who don't understand you can get free High Definition digital TV signals straight to your HD monitor using free over-the-air signals and an antenna; they think you have to pay money to a provider to get ABC, CBS, NBC, PBS, Fox, Telemundo, and Univision. No, those are free!

A great resource for numerous hints on how to save money on large and small purchases is Clark Howard, whose podcast, online community, e-mail newsletter, and written and video articles can be accessed at clark.com. I enjoy his podcast as I drive to and from work.

Retirement Account

If my older self could communicate to my younger self, I would tell myself to buy only used cars, and put the savings into retirement.

Retirement researchers are now saying that young people need to plan to put at least 15% of their earnings into retirement savings.

Retirement no-brainers you can implement:

You should absolutely contribute enough to your company 401(k) plan to capture the full company match, or else you are simply leaving money on the table

As a young person at the lower end of the salary scale, you should use the Roth 401(k) option, if it is available, because your current tax rates are lower than your future tax rates, as far as we know. With the Roth 401(k), you contribute after-tax money, but then in the distant future when you use it for retirement, you won't pay taxes on it (that's what the U.S. Federal Government promises, at any rate). The traditional 401(k) is tax-deferred; you get an immediate tax break on your contributions, but then your future withdrawals are taxed. With the Roth 401(k), you are pre-paying your tax, and it makes sense to do that when you are young and are facing lower tax rates. They will be higher later.

You can put $18,000 (as of 2016) into a 401(k) every year from payroll deduction only. You cannot write a check and put it into a 401(k). If you completely use up that $18,000, you can put $5,500 (as of 2016) into a Roth IRA, as long as your taxable income (AGI) is below $117,000, if unmarried.

Some of Clark Howard's preferred providers for Roth IRAs are Charles Schwab, Vanguard, Fidelity, and T. Rowe Price. I use Schwab and Vanguard.

Another excellent retirement savings vehicle is the Health Savings Account, or HSA. If you sign up for a High Deductible Health Plan (HDHP) at work, and it comes with an HSA attached, then you can put $3,350 as a single person per year into the HSA, and you get two tax benefits; you get to contribute pre-tax dollars, so it's a tax shelter, and you make future withdrawals tax-free so long as you spend the money on healthcare.

If you fill up the 401(k), the Roth IRA, and the HSA, and still want to invest more, you can certainly open a taxable account, and invest unlimited amounts of money, but it will be exposed to taxation on dividends, interest, and capital gains.

The 401(k), Roth IRA, and HSA retirement accounts are just empty containers that describe how the assets will be taxed; the more basic question is, how should a 20-something invest for retirement? What should into those containers?

The answer is they should invest aggressively, meaning mostly stocks from around the world. What disturbs me is learning that Millennials are fearful of the stock market, having watched their parents suffer through the 2000 "Tech Bubble" and 2008 "Great Recession" market crashes, in other words, they are anchoring their expectations to what they witnessed in 2000 and/or 2008.

The easy choice is to choose the "Target Date" retirement fund in your investment account appropriate to your retirement age, say, Target Date 2055 (39 years from today). If there is no such option, just buy the entire world's stock market with an ETF like Vanguard's Total World Stock ETF, symbol VT, and keep 5% or 10% in a bond fund, like Vanguard's Total Bond Market ETF, symbol BND. Or buy some US stocks with symbol VTI, and some International stocks with VEU. American investors usually have a home country bias (they are more heavily invested in the USA), and that might come back to harm us. Well-diversified portfolios do better over a long period of time. At least ¼ of your stocks could be non-US stocks, up to ½.

I don't mean to trivialize stock market declines and bear markets. They are nasty and dangerous. They can wreck the retirement plans of someone ten years or nearer to retirement. But, a 20-something has time on his or her side, four decades in which to recover and grow their assets. You simply need to own a lot of Prosperity assets at this age. If you keep to "safe" things like Money Market funds, inflation will steadily eat your savings away to nothing. In Appendix A, I do mention Tactical Asset Allocation techniques which manage portfolio risk and reduce drawdowns. An enterprising 20-something could employ Tactical Asset Allocation, and have a smoother ride to retirement; but it's admittedly more work, and not for everyone.

Surprise! Tactical Asset Allocation uses stock market charting techniques like the 200 day moving average described in Chapter 1. These strategies aim to get you out of stocks when the uptrend is broken and a price collapse is in progress, just as charting oil price trends will warn you of career risk.

Rent or Buy?

People in their 20s universally start out as renters, but then, after years of paying rent, many get tired of it and wonder if homeownership isn't a better idea. I became a homeowner at age 26, and I think I would do it again in the same way, but I am going to burst your bubble; real estate is not that great an investment. Over long periods of time, across many different markets, real estate appreciates at about 1% per year, so it's not that good of a standalone investment from a capital gains point of view. The real value of residential real estate is *the value of the place to live* the real estate investment provides, essentially *a service wrapped inside of a slowly-appreciating asset*. Also, having a mortgage may allow Federal tax deductions for mortgage interest and property taxes which might otherwise not be available to you; however, tax arguments alone should never be used to justify a home purchase.

If you are thinking about buying a home in your 20s, consider the following:

- Make use of a sophisticated online "rent or buy" calculators, such as the one published by the New York Times in 2014. Search online for it
- If the mortgage company qualifies you to borrow $X, then budget for much less than than $X, and shop for a house that will fit that payment. Don't try to stretch yourself around the max payment possible. You don't want to be mortgaged up to your neck. I have always felt very comfortable carrying a lighter monthly payment
- Never dig into your emergency fund to finance your home purchase

- Don't forget - budget for repairs, property taxes, utilities, homeowner's association fees

- Total housing spend should be no more than ¼ of your after-tax take-home pay

- Don't buy if the oil industry is entering a period of instability (see Chapter 1)

- If you think your employer might relocate you in the next few years, don't buy a house unless they have a nice relocation package where they will take much of the selling risk out of the equation by making an offer on your house

- If you've been hired into the industry during an upswing, and things are really hot and hopping, consider that you may be buying into a housing bubble. There are two responses to the possibility of a bubble:

  1. You may want to jump in and buy as a hedge against further inflation. Many Denver and Calgary residents who went elsewhere to work for years and have tried to come back home to live have found they have been totally priced out of those housing markets, due to price appreciation. They probably wished they'd have kept a rental property as a place to come home to

  2. You may want to wait a bubble out, and buy when prices moderate. Certainly in the aftermath of the oil price collapse of 2014 there has been home price moderation in some, but not all, markets. 1986 – 1987 was a great time to buy in oil towns; everyone was selling

- Back to the transportation theme - it may pay to buy or rent a more costly dwelling if you are able to take public transit, bike, or walk, and leave a car at home, or downsize the number of cars in your household. Do the math to see how it works out for you

One thing that worries me is Houston has clearly lost its edge as a truly low-cost place to live and raise a family. My first house was a bungalow on Timmons Lane, Bellaire, TX 77401. In 2016 Dollars, it cost $159,014. Of course, there is nothing at all in that location to be found for $159,014 any longer. You have to go very far out to find that price point. Before we bought, we rented a 1-BR apartment inside Loop 610 close to Greenway Plaza for $750 in 2016 Dollars. Today, the average rent in Houston is $1,200, and our original apartment is set to be demolished to make way for luxury apartments renting for many thousands of dollars per month.. There is a real housing affordability crisis that affects 20-something with no home equity particularly strongly.

Yes, the more expensive houses and apartments are built very nicely, compared to older construction practices. But that's a distraction and a temptation. If it's unaffordable to you, it doesn't matter how nice is it relative to what they used to offer in the past. If a property is 10% too expensive, then making it 10% nicer for the same money doesn't make it affordable; it's just nicer, but still unaffordable, so you should still walk away from the offer.

In summary, if you are fortunate enough to land a high-paying Oil & Gas job in your 20s, you need to anchor your spending expectations and budget as if you were a couple of notches lower on the economic scale. Fortunately, there is a simple way to do that, and that way is: payroll deduction. If the money never gets into your checking account, it's not there to spend.

First, do massive payroll deduction to build up your emergency fund, according to my recommendations in Chapter 3.

Second, after the emergency fund is built, go "all-in" as much as possible on the 401(k) and Roth IRA and HSA deductions, which altogether will allow you to save up to $26,850 for a single person in 2016. Being a very aggressive saver and investor early in life will knock back your spending. Don't worry, you'll get used to it. And that is precisely the point anyway, to knock back your spending.

If you save $26,850 every year for forty years, assuming a 3% real (inflation-adjusted) market return, you would end up with $2.02 million in today's Dollars, not inflated future Dollars. That would be a pretty good start to your retirement.

6 KIDS ARE EXPENSIVE!

So you got through your 20s, you're now in your late 20s, 30s, or 40s now. You've maybe bought a house, and you have one or more kids. You feel the pressure of all of the expenses! You may be wonder what you can do to meet your obligations, while still managing to keep your growing brood safe from what the Oil & Gas industry might throw your way, should a downturn strike.

Life Insurance

At this point in life, you absolutely need to protect your family from the loss of your income. I am not going to try to counsel you in a few pages here as to how much life insurance you should carry, but I will say that most people should seek out term life insurance, which only provides a death benefit, rather than a cash value life insurance, which builds up residual value over time, and can provide a tax sheltered retirement income stream.

If you haven't totally maxed-out the savings allowed by the IRS for your 401(k), IRA, and HSA, then why pursue the "cash-value life insurance as an investment" angle? If you have totally maxed out your tax-advantaged savings, and you just don't know what to do with all of your money, and if your taxable income is greater than $350,000 per year (threshold suggested by Clark Howard), or if you have estate planning problems because you're very affluent, then you can look at cash-value life insurance. But if you're that affluent, you don't need to be reading this book. You should be having a meeting with your wealth advisor, at your private club, or in your luxury residence.

Variable Universal Life (VUL) policies sound like a potential trap. Apparently the promises of "vanishing premiums" and "insurance policies that eventually pay for themselves" have not stood up to the financial market conditions of the post-Great Recession era, which have been characterized by lower and lower money market and bond interest rates, and since October 2014, by stock market volatility and a market trapped in a trading range. Insurance companies are some of the largest investors in the financial markets. If they can't make money, then their variable and variable universal policyholders can't attain the "illustrations" which were printed in marketing flyers, but which were not actually promised in the highly complex insurance contracts. Clark Howard gets plenty of calls from listeners whose Variable Universal Life policies blew up on them, and they have no value left in them (zero), even after making premium payments for a long while; and they have no insurance! The S&P 500 stock index lost 80% of its value during the Great Depression, but did not go to zero, and it came back, after a long while. Zero is really harsh compared to even a -80% decline. Zero means zero, forever!

If you are looking at cash value life insurance, it's probably best to limit your inquiry to Whole Life, a predictable, contractually-based agreement sometimes called "straight life" or "ordinary life".

Your life insurance, no matter what type you choose, should not be sole-sourced from your employer. You should get the vast majority of it on your own, through an insurance agent or broker. Why? Because you don't want your life insurance to vanish the moment you are laid-off. What if you were to sicken or have an accident and die while unemployed? Your family could become destitute.

Disability insurance

Every breadwinner in a family should have disability insurance, and so much the better if you can get it through an insurance agent or broker and not through your employer, for the reasons just cited for life insurance; you don't want a lay-off to wipe out your protection.

Doug Roufa, an independent insurance agent in the Houston area, managed to find a disability insurance policy for me, even though I was newly-unemployed, and most disability companies won't touch the unemployed. The argument was that I was a high-value consultant. It was an expensive policy, but good to have for the months I needed it. Doug is listed in

Appendix B.

K-12 school costs

The Kinkaid School is a top-tier private school in West Houston. The 2016-2017 tuition ranges from $20,500 annually for Pre-K to $25,000 annually for high school. Other high performing private schools in Houston can't be all that far behind.

Over the years, I have known people who send their kids to private school, which is their choice to make, but then they don't have an acceptable fall-back plan should they experience a catastrophic loss of family income. That is, they live in an area with what they consider to be unacceptable public schools.

I think the problem here is not that they send their children to private school, but that there is not an acceptable back-up plan if private school becomes unaffordable. The error was possibly in the real estate choice. I think it's safest if you choose to live in a school district with acceptable public schools, even if your kids still go to private.

Or maybe the error is in the parents' definition of what is "unacceptable". There is a difference between what is truly unacceptable - poor programs, low achievement, assaults, and bullying in the hallways - versus perceived unacceptability of their children having to attend school with kids from all races, religions, and socio-economic backgrounds, possibly in well-worn facilities. Some public schools are excellent. Some stink. You won't know until you take a really hard, close look at the individual campus.

Whatever you do, parents need a back-up plan in case of job loss. In my opinion, it's not acceptable to send your child or children at some large fraction of $25,000 apiece annually while the principal breadwinner is idle. Of course, the school would likely give financial aid, but a full ride? Paying out any significant amount during a period of unemployment for private school when public school is tuition-free is just so unsound. It sounds like a case of denial of the facts of unemployment. Yes, it's terrible to have to go from a great private school to a not-so-great public school. This very thing happened to me as a middle-schooler during 1973-1975 in Chicago, due to parental job loss and relocation. Evidently, I survived intact.

In all fairness, I should probably mention that home-schooling is also back-up plan to private school, but then that ties one parent to the home, and they might have to be out seeking work to provide in-fill income while the one who was laid-off is trying to get back on their feet.

Our family chose in 1992 to move into Cypress Fairbanks ISD, a very good suburban school district, and our two kids went to public school from K-12, and received excellent educations, and both went on to excellent colleges. Their high school, by the way, is "majority-minority" (largest ethnic group only 40% of total population), where 33% of kids get free or reduced price lunch, due to family poverty. By appearances, maybe not expected to be a good school, but in reality - a very good school.

College Costs

A similar logic can be applied to college education for your kids as was applied to K-12, above. That is - plan for the best, but don't be surprised by the worst.

What I specifically mean is, don't pile 100% of your college savings money into tax-advantaged college savings plans like the 529 plan, or the Coverdell plan. Why? Because once you put the funds in those plans, it is intended to be used on behalf of your child for educational purposes only. If the principal breadwinner loses his or her job, no one will care about sending the kid to Harvard or Stanford - the focus will be on keeping the lights on, people fed, and the house from being foreclosed on. In such a circumstance, UT or TAMU (any campus), UH, OU, LSU and other public colleges and universities start to look pretty good.

If you're saving for ambitions beyond public education, then do so in a regular bank savings account, or very conservative allocation in a regular taxable (in the parent's name) brokerage account. That way, if you keep your job in Oil & Gas, your student can indeed go to the more expensive college. If you lose you job at the wrong moment, as I did, you can immediately re-purpose these excess funds to meet family survival needs.

I would advise against putting any college savings in the student's name as a way to avoid Federal income tax. This is because in the Free Application for Federal Student Aid (FAFSA) computation, students savings count more heavily than parents savings, and will ultimately reduce the amount of an financial aid award from the school. You don't want to win a minor tax victory, but lose the college financing war.

Please review Chapter 4, and think about ways to reduce the cost of college. For example; living at home, not on campus; attending the first two years at community college while living at home; academic and sports scholarships; ROTC programs.

How it played out for us

I mentioned my daughter in the Introduction to this book. She was a Senior in High School when I was laid-off in 2015. For eighteen years we parents had been piling funds into a 529 college savings account, but also into regular savings. We were preparing to send her to a costly private college, possibly Rice University, or maybe out-of-state tuition for Georgia Tech.

As the oil industry softened in late 2014, I think she may have picked up on the subconscious vibe in the household and the dinner-table talk about how things were going at work, possibly from friends also, and she changed her ambition from attending private college to attending the University of Houston's Honors College, which admitted her for Fall 2015.

And then, unexpectedly, I was laid-off in March 2015. But no longer was the entire pile of college money accumulated needed to send her to UH, only the 529 account half. The equally large portion of regular bank savings were still in her parents' name, free to use for any purpose.

Things worked out well. I have been one of lucky few to return to work full-time in Oil & Gas, and the half of her college savings which is not going to be tapped for college could be used for graduate school, a wedding, a car, a down-payment on her first house, or her parents' retirement. Or, given that Oil & Gas employment is still very weak and unstable, we may still have to eat these funds in coming years. But the flexibility is there, because they were not tied-up in tax-advantaged vehicles to begin with.

By the way, she loves UH.

Are parents obligated to pay for a child's college education?

Because of the extremely high cost of college, there is a debate raging about the priority of college savings versus retirement savings.

In my opinion, there is no debate. Retirement has to come first. Parents will someday have to retire, and many times retirement is completely involuntary, even if workers say they are going to "work until they die". Some people are too sick to work. Or, workers get fired and then no one wants to hire them again; age discrimination is a real, under-reported problem. You can't take out a loan to retire on; ultimately, after work ends your retirement income stream must come from Social Security, Medicare, pensions, savings and investments, insurance cash value or annuities, inheritances, home equity… and other public assistance grants and gifts from family and friends. There are no other sources.

If parents have not done a good job of saving for the children's higher education, I realize this implies that children don't go to college, or they accumulate large amounts of debt in order to attend, or they give some years of their life to the military (ROTC). Yes, these are the hard facts. But the alternative; parents becoming destitute in old age; is worse.

Retirement

Therefore, throughout the years when the kids are at home, parents have to keep up retirement savings begun back when they were in their 20s (Chapter 5). It would be extremely helpful to know with more precision how much to save for retirement, and not over-save and "starve" competing family needs, so at this stage of life parents should be using retirement planning tools, available free online from discount brokerages like Charles Schwab, Vanguard, Fidelity, or T. Rowe Price. If these are too overwhelming or confusing, you should seek out professional help from a financial planner who can look at your entire financial situation and life goals, and make appropriate recommendations for you which will allow you to hit your goals with the least amount of risk. I have much more information on this topic in Appendix A - Advisors and Strategies.

In Chapter 5 for 20-somethings, I suggested one possible asset allocation as being a mostly stock allocation, just the entire world's stock market with an ETF like Vanguard's Total World Stock ETF, symbol VT, and 5% or 10% in a bond fund, like Vanguard's Total Bond Market ETF, symbol BND. Well, this is probably too aggressive by the time you are old enough to have a family with kids. You should be adding more bonds, and possibly a slice of Alternative Investments as well, mentioned in the next chapter, Chapter 7 for Pre-retirees (managed futures, REITS, precious metals, non-oil non-gas commodities, tactical). The easiest answer by far, however, is to stick with the Target Date retirement fund you started with in your 20s.

Elderly destitution is a problem that is likely to become worse and worse in coming years, due to the double-whammy effects of the 2000 Tech Bubble and 2008 Great Recession stock market declines, the loss of defined-benefit retirement plans (traditional pensions), low savings rates, low market interest rates, poor investor education and behavior ("buy high and sell low"), and Social Security and Medicare solvency issues on the horizon.

In the next chapter, we will delve headlong into the difficult challenge Oil & Gas workers face in avoiding elder destitution as they head into the final stretch of years after the kids are gone, and before full retirement can be celebrated.

7 PRE-RETIREMENT EMPTY NESTERS

This is an easy chapter for me to write, as my wife and I are mid-50s, empty nesters, pre-retirement.

The real challenge for pre-retirees who get laid-off from a high-paying Oil & Gas job is that suddenly the assumptions underlying the retirement plan get shot to hell. The huge temptation for someone in this situation who has gotten "retired" with a reduced pension, or a generous severance package, is to capitulate and declare, "Ah, I'm tired of the rat race, I'm just going to retire. I have enough money".

They may very well live well enough from age 55 or 60 for fifteen or twenty years.

And then… in the last 5 or 10 years of their life… when they are in poor health, low spirits, and are in greatest need of a dignified and honorable retirement… they completely run out of money. You know, being broke and out of money for ten days must be stressful… but for ten years? When you're sick and old? How terrible.

Unfortunately, I have lived through this very scenario with my own Father. He ran out of money, I'm not sure when, maybe a couple of years before his death. He never communicated openly to me about money; he was obviously ashamed, but the non-communication made matters worse. He was unable to pass along any assets, other than his house, to his widow. Our step-mother now lives precariously on Social Security and Medicare alone, facing an uncertain future. I am certain this is not what Dad would've intended as his future vision for his loved ones. And yet… it happened. His experience, our family experience, is precisely what powers me to write with passion and conviction about financial planning. It is what drove me back to school five months after his death to earn the Chartered Retirement Planning Counselor[SM] or CRPC® designation, while still working full-time in Oil & Gas as a Geophysicist.

So let's back up and examine what kind of planning you should be doing now, as a pre-retiree, to avoid a bad end later in life.

The plan is the central element

Would you take off and fly an airplane a long distance without a flight plan? Of course not. Yet, that is what people do with their lives. They take off and "wing it" and do things without any detailed fact-based, math-based idea of where they are going, what the destination looks like, when they might arrive, and how to react when conditions change.

You alone or you and your financial advisor must do a detailed retirement plan during the pre-retirement phase. Actually, it's best to begin much earlier in life than this. I was planning the broad outlines of my retirement at age 25 with a hand-calculator and paper in the 1980s before I owned a spreadsheet program. By age 40 I was using online planning tools. So I have known how my retirement would play out in some detail for fifteen years, and in fuzzy detail for thirty years - the entire length of my working life. Amazingly, I have not been far off. My initial hen-scratchings in pencil, buried in a file folder, ended up close to reality because over a long period of time, stock market returns revert toward certain averages, and these were the averages I used in 1986. The math of compound interest is known to any high-schooler who has done pre-Calculus, done with a few keystrokes on a business or scientific calculator. But it's even easier now, it's all done for you using online planning tools, all for free.

There are many online retirement planning tools available from the American Association of Retired Persons (AARP), Fidelity Investments, T. Rowe Price, Vanguard, and Charles Schwab. I have been a Schwab client for a long time, and I have used their retirement planning tool for years.

All of these tools will ask you the same or very similar broad questions:

- How old are you?
- How long do you think you might live?
- At what age do you want to retire?
- Are you married / partnered?

- How much do you and/or your partner have saved for retirement now?

- How much do you and/or your partner save for retirement every year?

- How much will you want to spend in retirement?

- What kind of asset allocations do you plan to use before and after retirement?

- What is your marginal tax bracket?

- When do you plan to take Social Security?

- What will your Social Security benefit be?

- Will you have a pension? How much? When does it start? Single or two-life annuity?

- Will you inherit any money before you retire?

- Inflation - the program will "bake in" to their forecasts some kind of inflation assumption

The best programs will do a "Monte Carlo" analysis, where they will do multiple retirement income projections using hundreds or even thousands of different possible stock market scenarios, hence the term "Monte Carlo" - the scenarios all result from the computer program doing "coin flips" using random number generators. Less sophisticated programs will just give you one set of numbers. I don't favor this approach. It's too simplistic.

The retirement plan will allow you to estimate your lifetime retirement income. The following is a hypothetical example of a conclusion the planning process would allow you to make:

"Based on past stock market and inflation history, and based on how much I will save until I retire, and how much pension I will accrue, I have a 95% chance of being able to spend a total of $125,000 in retirement from age 65 to age 95, and I will be able to give myself a raise each year to compensate for inflation, and my heirs might inherit between $250,000 and $1,000,000 at my death."

That simple but complete statement, coming out of a solid Monte Carlo analysis, is so much better than "winging it". Having that level of understanding will allow you to avoid what happened to my Dad.

Re-do the plan every year

Every year, on my birthday, I re-do my plan. It takes only a few minutes. I idea is, as you get closer and closer to retirement, the uncertainty gets less and less. You will either feel more confident and better about your future, or you will see the plan "going sideways" and this may light a fire underneath you to make changes in your life.

By "going sideways" I mean the plan will tell you if you're at risk of running out of money in your later years. If you have less than a 50% chance of reaching the oldest age you might live to with your required level of income, then you have a problem. If you have a 95% or greater chance of reaching the oldest age you might live to with your required level of income, then you're pretty secure.

If you get laid-off, you must re-do your plan immediately

Retiring early has a huge impact on your retirement plan, especially since before age 65 you may have to buy very expensive health and long-term care insurance on the private market. Your plan has to fund additional years of retirement, yet it has lost years of savings and investment.

As stated earlier, you cannot simply declare, "Ah, I'm tired of the rat race, I'm just going to retire. I have enough money". If you re-do your detailed retirement plan with the new post-layoff assumptions, and you like the numbers you see, then by all means retire if you want to. You would've earned it. But you have to do the planning first, or else you may run out of fuel before you land your plane.

Sometimes, people save too much, work too long, maybe continuing to work while they have a serious, painful, exhausting illness. A retirement plan can also tell you when to pack it in, so you can enjoy whatever time remains to you on this Earth with your family and friends. As First Lady Barbara Bush wisely said at Wellesley College Commencement on June 1, 1990:

> "For several years, you've had impressed upon you the importance to your career of dedication and hard work. And, of course, that's true. But as important as your obligations as a doctor, a lawyer, a business leader will be, you are a human being first. And those human connections --- with spouses, with children, with friends -- are the most important investments you will ever make.

At the end of your life, you will never regret not having passed one more test, winning one more verdict, or not closing one more deal. You will regret time not spent with a husband, a child, a friend, or a parent."

If your retirement plan blew up due to getting laid-off, what can you do?

Your options really come down to:

- Keep working at something
- Retire later
- Spend less
- Save more

Oil & Gas people live a pretty good life. In other words, there is often fat to trim off of a lifestyle, maybe a lot.

Keeping the integrity of your retirement plan is more important than:

- A big house that no longer has any children in it
- Second homes you can no longer afford - choose which one you want to live in, and sell the other one
- Luxury cars or multiple cars
- Boats and Monster Trucks
- Supporting grown children and other relatives
- Excessive consumer spending supported by debt

I refer you back to Chapter Two and Dave Ramsey's "Baby Steps". When your retirement plan gets whacked by a layoff, you really have to do some soul-searching and decide what are your <u>needs</u> in life versus your <u>wants</u>.

Making Capital Gains lemonade out of lemons

Way back in Chapter 2, I suggested that workers could use taxable brokerage accounts as part of their retirement savings, in order to have more spending options should they get laid off before age 59-½.

If you find yourself laid-off, even if only temporarily, and your taxable income for the tax year is low, you can take the Capital Gains on the stock in your taxable brokerage accounts, and you could potentially pay ZERO Capital Gains tax. Then you can re-buy the same stock 31 days later and complete "disappear" your Capital Gains problem. Check with your tax advisor before you do it. This kind of tactic makes a taxable brokerage account perform a bit more like a Roth IRA.

Pitfalls to avoid

Over-concentration in company stock

It's very common for Oil & Gas people to accumulate a lot of shares of stock issued by their employers. It is not unheard of for company stock to plummet in value, or even go to zero:

"OKLAHOMA CITY, March 22, 2016 (Reuters) - Nearly 15 years

since Enron's collapse decimated the retirement accounts of its employees, hundreds of thousands of U.S. energy workers remain precariously exposed to big, concentrated bets on company stock in their 401(k) retirement plans.

The slide in oil prices to their lowest levels in over a decade wiped out several billion dollars of retirement wealth in the energy sector in the past year. The losses may prove temporary for companies that successfully navigate the crisis, but tens of thousands of employees of struggling firms may see much of their nest eggs gone for good.

In Oklahoma and Texas, workers are delaying retirement plans, surrendering trucks, cars and land in personal bankruptcy cases, or just praying oil prices will recover.

'I just didn't see it coming,' said John Thompson, 57, who was laid off in February from Oklahoma City-based SandRidge Energy Inc. SandRidge shares, which peaked above $65 in 2008, are now worth 10 cents apiece. 'Because of this, I'm not retiring any time soon.'"

Don't even tempt fate. Whenever you get an opportunity to sell company stock you have been granted, definitely do so whenever the amount of company stock you own exceeds 10% of your total portfolio value. That way, if it goes to zero, you still have 90% of your money. Does that sounds like a good idea? You are not morally obligated to own any company stock at all. If you want to, sell it all as soon as you are allowed to.

Referring back to Chapter One and the discussion of oil prices and charting techniques - if you see whichever index matters to you; your company stock share price, or oil prices, or natural gas prices, or energy ETFs (XLE, XES) below their 200-day moving averages, it may really be a good time to sell most or even all of your company stock holdings. When current prices cross below the 200-day moving average of prices, that's a long-term bearish indicator, it indicates a risk of further declines.

Corollary: over-involved with Oil & Gas industry stock

Here's an interesting tidbit from MarketWatch, December 28, 2015:

> Peter Lynch wants you to know that his ideas are being misquoted widely.
>
> "I've never said, 'If you go to a mall, see a Starbucks and say it's good coffee, you should call Fidelity brokerage and buy the stock,'" Lynch says, some 25 years after his retirement from running Magellan Fund was front-page news.
>
> What's wrong with the popular-wisdom version of his ideology, which is usually cited as "invest in what you know"? It leaves out the role of serious fundamental stock research. "People buy a stock and they know nothing about it," he says. "That's gambling and it's not good."

There are many, many thousands of Oil & Gas workers who assume that they "know" what is going on in the industry, and they invest heavily in industry stock, even if not in their own employer stock. But I agree with Peter Lynch, it's gambling, and it's not good.

There used to be a financial radio program in Houston on KTEK 1100

AM, called "Market Wrap with Moe Ansari". Moe got dropped because KTEK is a daytime-only AM station, and the scheduling did not work out. But, it's a fun and informative show, and I still get it via live streaming or podcast, though beware - it is an hour-long commercial. But when it was on the radio in Houston, the Houston listeners used to call in even during the slow-motion 2015 industry crash, and ask, "Moe... what do you think of Transocean? What do you think of Baker-Hughes?"

You just know the Houston callers were in the industry themselves, their jobs were all hanging by threads, and they wanted to place wagers on companies whose fortunes were just about exactly the same as their own at-risk employers. Does that sound like a good idea?

And let's say you did have some unique "insider knowledge" which would allow you to buy or sell a company's stock at an opportune time. That's called Insider Trading, and it's against Federal law. Feel free to join Martha Stewart's ranks in Federal prison (she traded ImClone shares illegally), but as for me, no thank you.

In fact, maybe Upstream Oil & Gas employees should consider buying stocks which negatively correlate with Upstream Oil & Gas stocks, like Refiners, or Airlines. When hydrocarbon prices go down, Refiners and Airliners can benefit.

Taking Social Security too early

Many Oil & Gas early retirees take Social Security early, but then have it in their minds to keep working part-time or on contract prior to truly full retirement.

Then, they get the shock - they lose up to 50% of their Social Security benefits due to taxation because they earn more than the Earned Income limit, which was only $15,720 in 2015. That's a minimum wage level, if you were to earn it out over a year.

If you plan to work as an Oil & Gas consultant in retirement, do not take Social Security prior to your Full Retirement Age (FRA). The FRA gradually changes from 65 for those born in 1937 and earlier to 67 for those born in 1961 and later. It slides by two months for every year change in the birth year. Go to www.ssa.gov to see what your Full Retirement Age (FRA) is. Actually, at the same time, you should sign up to get your official estimate of retirement benefits, either online or in the US Mail.

Missing Medicare sign-up deadlines

If you miss the age 65 Medicare sign-up date, you will be assessed with increased Medicare premiums for the rest of your life. Start looking into the sign-up process several months before you turn 65.

The wrong asset allocation

Some pre-retirees exist on the extremes. Some people are fear-driven and want "safety", so they keep all of their retirement money in cash and CDs, which pay very little now. They have no hope of keeping up with inflation over the possible forty remaining years of their lifetime. Their perception of safety and risk is skewed; the real risk which they haven't addressed is that they will run out of money because they are holding a no-growth asset.

On the other extreme are greed-driven people, who want to be 100% in stock, maybe even leveraged, so they get as rich as possible. They forget that a global stock portfolio decreased by 40% in 2008, and took until 2013 to come back to par. A 40% wealth hit on the day before you retire is a terrible blow. This is called "sequence of returns risk", a situation where you have a serious market decline in the years just before retirement or in early retirement, creating a heightened risk of running out of money in your old age. Delaying retirement by five years, from 65 to 70, assuming there would even be a job available for you to do and you were still healthy enough and able to work safely, would be a huge effort. Don't forget that age discrimination is rampant in many industries, including Oil & Gas.

I have gone through a personal journey in how I view asset allocation, which I detail in the "Investing Style" section of Appendix A: Advisors and Strategies. My journey is my own; my destination will not be your destination; but I think it's useful to read, because it shows how my thinking as a laid-off pre-retiree changed dramatically over a short period of time (19 months) as I confronted sequence of returns risk.

One thing I have learned from Meb Faber's book, "Global Asset Allocation" is that most of the asset allocation strategies out there, in the end, over a long period of time, perform somewhat similarly. The point is, once you have found the asset allocation strategy that fits you and your phase of life, it's best to stick with it through thick and thin. Also, investment costs matter very much in how a strategy performs over time. There are now very low cost ETFs and mutual funds that can form the basis of your asset allocation, that trade for less than $9 or for free at major discount stock brokerage houses.

I have pointed out two example "wrong" pitfall asset allocations (all cash vs. all stocks), but what asset allocation is right for you is way beyond the scope of this short book. You will have to do some more reading. I recommend Meb Faber's book Global Asset Allocation, listed in Appendix B. Also see the webpages for Fidelity Investments, T. Rowe Price, Vanguard, and Charles Schwab for self-help resources for investors. Or, seek out a genuine financial advisor (Appendix A).

Is life insurance an "investment"?

If you haven't read it already, please circle back to Chapter Six and read what I wrote about Life Insurance, especially highly-complex insurance policies like Variable Universal Life (VUL) which are heavily pitched as "investments".

Life insurance products are fine if they are presented appropriately, as part of the balanced, holistic lifetime retirement and estate plan put together by a financial planner who is acting in your best interests. Almost every pre-retiree needs life insurance. That's an undeniable fact.

Life insurance products are not fine if they are presented out-of-context with your needs, if no comprehensive financial planning has been done, and if they are being pitched using "illustrations", optimistic what-if scenarios which do not appear in the actual binding insurance contract language. I would say further that if an "investment plan" is being proposed to you that is 100% insurance, and does not have you participating in the future economic growth of the United States and International regions through global stock and bond ownership, you are being sold an inadequate plan.

Insurance is a financial derivative, you don't own the underlying assets.
I am reminded of the Charles Schwab slogan: "Own Your Tomorrow".
Isn't that a good idea? I swear by it.

Remember - follow the money. If the so-called "financial planner" works for a life insurance company, he or she has a monthly quota to meet. They have to close a given number of life insurance contracts in a month, or else they don't get their commissions, or they may even get fired. You can bet they will bend the truth to the breaking point, parse words, and do almost anything to get you to sign.

If you went to a butcher, how much beef would they tell you to buy? They would not be pitching salads or oatmeal, that's for sure.

If you only shop from a life insurance company for your retirement plan, how much insurance do you think they will tell you to buy?

I think you are better served working with an advisor who offers many different kinds of products, including life insurance, which can be assembled into a portfolio customized to meet your specific needs.

Do you really want an annuity?

When I left Amoco in 1994, they started sending me pension checks. $41.21 per month for the rest of my life. Now I get the monthly check from BP.

I actually love the idea that I will get $41.21 per month for the rest of my life. I love the reliability aspect of annuities.

But if an annuity salesman comes to you today, sniffing out the fact that you just received a giant lump sum severance or retirement payment from your former employer, are you sure you want to turn it into an annuity? Remember - follow the money. What they want you to do maybe isn't what is in your best interest.

I ask that because interest rates are at historic lows, and I mean historic. We may never see low interest rates like this again in our lifetimes, after this lengthy post-2008 Financial Crisis "ZIRP / NIRP" (zero interest rate policy / negative interest rate policy) period finally ends someday. Annuity contracts are based on interest rates. Are you sure you want to lock in a very large chunk of your money at lifetime historic low interest rates?

What will you do if inflation picks up again? How will you be able to continue your retirement spending if you are not participating in growing "prosperity" assets like US and International stocks, or some "inflation hedge" assets like TIPS bonds (U.S. Treasury Inflation Protected Securities), or alternative investments, like precious metals or real estate?

Don't take me the wrong way - I may buy an annuity someday, but only as part of a balanced, well-constructed retirement and estate plan.

The proper use of "alternative investments" and gold

Just above I mentioned alternative investments like precious metals or real estate as possible hedges, or protections, against a future uptick in inflation. But I specifically did not mention a broad-basket of commodities as something to own. That was on purpose.

A broad-basket of commodities ETF like USCI is 55% correlated with an oil industry ETF like XLE (2010-2016). That's because these broad-baskets contain Oil & Gas futures contracts. Didn't we just conclude that we don't want to add Oil & Gas risk to our investable assets?

Silver metal, however, is only 35% correlated with the oil industry (SLV vs. XLE, 2006-2016). Gold is even lower, only 21% correlated with the oil industry (GLD vs. XLE, 2006-2016).

Remember, as Oil & Gas employees we do not want to own things which are highly correlated with our employment and prosperity. The smaller the correlation percentage, the better. So, I am skipping the broad-basket of commodities, which includes Oil & Gas, and instead thinking about gold (GLD, IAU, or SGOL), silver (SIVR or SLV), base metals (DBB), agricultural commodities (DBA).

Be careful about the timber ETF (WOOD). It is 75% correlated with XLE. Isn't that strange?

Other alternative investment classes would be Real Estate Investment Trusts or REITS. A couple of sample ETFs would be SCHH (U.S. REIT) or RWO (Global REIT).

How much of these alternative investments might an investor consider? At an American Association of Individual Investors Meeting in Houston in January 2016, I heard Christine Benz, Director of Personal Finance at Morningstar, suggest up to 10% into REITS, if you want REITS.

Invesco Ltd. has an educational campaign called "Goodbye 60/40, Hello 50/30/20". 50/30/20 means 50% stocks, 30% bonds, and 20% alternative investments. That 20% could be 10% REITS and 10% metals and non-oil, non-gas commodities.

My personal opinion is that you could put 5% - 10% into precious metals and/or non-oil, non-gas commodities. There are some mainstream providers thinking the same way. Charles Schwab's Intelligent Portfolios robo-advisor puts about 5% of an investor's assets into gold (GLD). Morningstar Lifetime Allocation Indexes suggest a 4% allocation to commodities for all investors. On the other extreme, Harry Browne's Permanent Portfolio (HBPP, Appendix A) calls for 25% gold, which is just a huge, huge slice. But it's useful as an upper limit in a way, it shows that even the most extremely gold-tilted but also a well-known and at times even admired portfolio is "only" 25% gold. Any calls for more than 25% gold and other precious metals should just be rejected out of hand. Commodities expert Doug Eberhardt further suggests a precious metals holding which is ¾ gold, ¼ silver.

More thoughts on gold - some Oil & Gas workers are very conservative people, and some of these most conservative folks adhere to a narrative that the United States is headed towards a economic collapse and hyperinflation in the long run, and that the only "safe" investment to own is gold, because U.S. Federal Reserve notes (FRNs, or what we call "money") are going to become highly devalued in the future. I don't know if they are right or wrong. I don't disagree or agree. But I still insist that even if you are totally pessimistic about the U.S. currency you limit your gold purchases to the Permanent Portfolio's 25% gold allocation.

Then there is the other problem about gold, and that is, is it fairly priced today? The long-term average price of gold in 2016 Dollars is about $483, or 2x the Consumer Price Index. Recently it is trading around $1270. That does not sound "cheap" to me. I like to buy things cheap. This is especially important for gold, because it pays no interest, no dividends. All of your gain depends on what you bought and sold it for. I am watching gold carefully, but I am not too excited about it at these prices.

One way to buy commodities is through "managed futures" mutual funds, where the fund managers take long positions and short positions in commodities and metals contracts, which requires a lot of expertise. That way they make money whether commodities and metals are going up or down in price. Then you don't worry about whether gold or other commodities are cheap or expensive. The managed futures guys only try to ride the trend. I own the LCSAX managed futures mutual fund from LoCorr Funds. The problem is, it's costly. It has a high expense ratio, and it has a high tax impact, because it has large distributions. But I only own a little slice. Managed futures funds are relatively new, I'm watching mine carefully to see if I like them over the long term.

Not all bonds are created equal

Investors have been going to longer and longer duration bonds (like Long Term U.S. Treasury Bonds) and to riskier High Yield ("Junk") bonds in order to try to get some more return on their investment. But this can be risky.

High Yield bonds got hammered with a -21.4% return in 2008 during the

Financial Crisis, and in 2015 experienced a -1.4% return. These were caused by defaults on bond interest payments, in 2015 many were due to shale loan defaults.

U.S. Long Term Treasury bonds had a -12.05% return in 2009, a -13.03% return in 2013, and a -1.54% return in 2015. The U.S. Government did not default; the poor performance was caused by market changes in interest rates.

A diversified portfolio of bonds, on the other hand, representing the Total Bond Market, had a -2.26% return in 2013, but no problems in 2008/2009 or 2015.

Bonds are very important to have in your portfolio, but the bulk of them should be high quality, intermediate term bonds. Not very long terms, and not high yield, high risk bonds either.

A state of denial

If little or none of what I've written in this Chapter makes any sense to you, or if it bores, bothers, or confuses you, and you just want to stop thinking about retirement, I think you're in a place where you need professional guidance. You need to get your retirement plan done, with help if necessary. I discuss how to distinguish real financial advisors from fake financial advisors in the "A real financial advisor can help you" section of Appendix A: Advisors and Strategies.

Other resources

I have only lightly touched on the many thorny issues surrounding retirement planning. I recommend that you delve further into the topic. A very lightweight but informative book in an easy-to-read FAQ format is "The Charles Schwab Guide to Finances After Fifty", by Carrie Schwab-Pomerantz and Joanne Cuthbertson.

Chapter 8 – Concluding Thoughts

The goal of financial planning

You have just read a financial planning book, but the last words in this very brief final chapter will serve to emphasize the point that the goal of financial planning is not about money.

The goal of financial planning is allow you to live your life. Financial planning is an enabler to a human life well lived, a life which has physical, mental, emotional, spiritual, family, and social dimensions.

Therefore, if you ever find the entire process of personal financial planning detracting from your life as a whole, creating more worry and more work for you, maybe you should consider changing how you approach the task.

Simplify and automate

Many individuals end up with dozens of securities and funds, scattered over many different accounts. Why not consolidate accounts where allowed by tax law, and consolidate all of your various stocks, bonds, mutual funds, and ETFs into a few or even one fund, like a target date retirement fund, or an asset allocation fund, or maybe you could let a robo-advisor automatically rebalance your account, rather than you having to do it. I mean – if you own ten U.S. stock mutual funds, you're probably getting S&P500-like performance, so why not just own one S&P500 mutual fund and be done with it?

Get help

Find advice and help from a financial professional. See my Appendices A and B for advice and references. You can even hire an advisor just to consult with you on specific questions, and you can pay them by the hour or by the job, and they won't try to sell you anything except their expertise. Maybe you just want to get a periodic check-up on your finances and your plan, and you don't need help on an on-going basis.

Be patient with yourself

If you have a long way to go to get to where you want to be, then it helps to be patient with yourself. It maybe took you years to get into the situation you are in, it may take months or years to get back out.

Think of financial planning objectives as long-term projects. Day-by-day, month-by-month, year-after-year, just work your plan. Keep saving, keep reducing debt, keep learning about how to invest. If you keep at it and don't give up, you will get to your goals, eventually. Here's an inspiring anecdote related by a Houston-area financial advisor, as closely as I can recall it:

> "I was having a portfolio review meeting with a client. The man suddenly started to cry! I asked him, 'What's wrong?' He replied, choking back the tears, 'I never, <u>ever</u> thought I'd be this wealthy.'"

Best Wishes

Those of us who have been in Oil & Gas for a long time know that it can be frustrating, even terrifying at times, but it can be very rewarding as well. The most rewarding part of this industry are the people in it. So, enjoy the ride, and the people you are journeying with. You will be rewarded financially, and also by the friendships made.

Appendix A – Advisors and Strategies

A real financial advisor can help you

If you're not a financial person, some of the topics in this book may be confusing to you, or maybe you understand them just fine, but you feel hesitant about actually taking actions related to your own finances.

It's one thing to think theoretically about what you should do with your money - it's another thing entirely to place a big stock trade maybe worth as much as a really nice car, then watch the price sink after you've bought the stock, or soar after you've sold it.

I am going to admit right up front that I have a portion, more than half, of my assets under management with a fee-based money manager. Even though I am an educated and informed investor, the difficulty is not with my intelligence, the difficulty is with my emotions. We've had considerable financial market turmoil since October 2014, and having some of my assets under management allows me to relax and focus on the rest of my life.

An advisor can provide "behavioral coaching", and talk you through the emotional roller-coasters that investing consists of. If you really don't understand investing, and many people do not, then even more reason to rely on an advisor. And don't feel badly if you consider yourself a personal finance newbie; this is a field with a huge body of knowledge.

How do you find a trustworthy financial advisor?

I think it's important to ask several important questions:

1. How do they get compensated?
2. Do they have a fiduciary responsibility towards you?
3. Training and designations
4. Do they make abrupt, incomplete, out-of-context recommendations?
5. Do they possess the appropriate licenses?
6. Your investment styles have to match

Compensation

The compensation question is critical. If they get compensated on commission, for selling you products, they are going to tend to push product in front of your face, and they might push whatever earns them the most money, even if it's not a good fit to your needs. This is not to say that you can't get good service and results from a commission compensation model, but it's more problematic. On the other hand, fee-based compensation means that you pay the advisor a fee, usually a percentage of the amount of money that is being managed by them. A typical fee is 1% of assets under management (AUM), but that 1% is under a lot of pressure now, with the recent rise of "robo-advisors", and they are probably headed lower in the future. Advisors are also doing more advising work on a turn-key basis, as consultants paid to solve a particular financial planning problem, but not paid on an on-going basis.

Do they put your interests first?

Also important is whether the advisor is acting as a fiduciary, which means are they acting in your best interests. You should ask them for a written statement which fully discloses their working relationship with you.

Training and designations

I would be suspicious of anyone who proposes to manage my money who does not have an undergraduate or graduate degree from a well-known accredited university in business administration, finance, accounting, or economics (BA, BS, BBA, MS, MBA). All kinds of characters end up in the gargantuan financial services industry, many of them unqualified. At least the academic degree is a partial filter against incompetence.

Beyond the academic degree, there are some professional designations you should seek out in a financial advisor. Below is a very short and incomplete list of the designations one can earn in the industry:

Accredited Asset Management Specialist, or AAMS®

Accredited Portfolio Management advisor, or APMA®

Accredited Wealth Management advisor, or AWMA®

Certified Financial Planner, or CFP®

Certified Investment Management Analyst, or CIMA®

Chartered Financial Analyst, or CFA®

Chartered Retirement Planning Counselor, or CRPC®

Of this list, the CFP® is the designation considered the most comprehensive for personal financial planners. Note, these designations are registered trademarks, it is illegal for a person to use these after their name if they don't actually possess the certification. They can be sued by the issuing organizations.

Even if the planner has wonderful training and designations, they might still not exhibit professional behaviors. Going to a financial planner is a lot like going to the doctor. In the case of the doctor, they have to take a very detailed personal medical history and do a comprehensive physical and also some diagnostic tests before deciding on a plan of action, and the appropriate plan of action might have many diverse elements in it (diet, exercise, elimination of smoking and drinking, personal safety practices, medication, surgery, or doing nothing). So if the financial planner doesn't take a detailed personal history, doesn't spend time doing any analysis, and just quickly gives you a recommendation to do just one thing very suddenly or abruptly, and if this "thing" is expensive and illiquid (you can't get your money back easily), and especially if they apply strong "closing techniques": like trying to create an artificial sense of urgency tied to their quota dates, or applying guilt or shame, or trying to tie into a political narrative or conspiracy theory, or if they exploit an affiliation (Bernie Madoff ripped-off a lot of fellow synagogue members) - then you are being manipulated. Walk away.

Even if you are in a bad financial state currently, it took you a long time to get there, and it will take months or years to get out of it. There is no need to panic, and no use in panicking, unless you have a truly emergent situation, for example, your home is being foreclosed on, or the IRS is trying to collect on unpaid back taxes. But really, in those cases, you need a person who is CPA and an Attorney, not a financial advisor.

If the so-called advisor gives you a narrow recommendation, like they only want you to buy an annuity, or only certain stocks or bonds, or only life insurance, or only invest in real estate, then you know you are dealing with a one-trick pony fake planner; a salesman.

A real planner is going to:

1. Take a detailed family financial history
2. Do a considerable amount of customized analysis
3. Help you with budgeting and control of expenses
4. Devise improvements to the way you currently handle your taxes
5. Help you plan for higher education for your children
6. Help you plan for all of the your insurance needs - life, health, disability
7. Coordinate with and maximize your employer benefits (not just try to replace them with his or her own products)
8. Advise you when to take Social Security

9. Help you to navigate the many traps involved in Social Security and Medicare

10. Advise you all of your short, intermediate, and long-term savings and investment strategies

11. Point you in the right direction concerning estate planning and passing on your assets according to your wishes

12. Talk you through it when the going gets tough

If the person you're engaging is not doing all of these things, and just wants you to buy something from them - move on. You're being sold.

Licensure

Any persons you deal with should be licensed by the Financial industry Regulatory Authority, or FINRA. You can easily verify whether your prospective planner hold FINRA licenses by going to brokercheck.finra.org and entering their name and zipcode. Typical licenses are the Series 7 and Series 63. If they are a Supervisor, they will have a Series 24. If you can't find them at all at FINRA, you should be concerned.

Don't get emotionally tied to a Financial Advisor

Of course we want to have friendly, courteous, open, transparent business transactions with a financial advisor. But, at the same time, if our needs change, we should not hesitate to change. I know that's a tough one. I had to make a change myself, and it was emotional hard for me. I asked the new advisor if he could please handle all aspects of the move, because it was too emotionally hard on me to contact my old advisor. I did thank the old advisor for his past service, and I think highly of him. It was purely a business decision.

Yes, be friendly with your advisor, but don't try to be friends. Your family and real friends will be there for you when the chips are down, the advisor maybe not. If there is a money exchange going on, after all, genuine friendship probably does not exist.

Investing style

I started investing in 1986 with well-known providers like USAA, T. Rowe Price, and Charles Schwab. From that date onward, I held a mixture of stock and bond mutual funds. I was a relatively aggressive investor, but along with everyone else I experienced the withering market declines of the Tech Bubble and the Great Recession.

In 2014, I started to become conscious of the fact that I was possibly no more than ten years away from retirement, and I started to become interested in strategies to control volatility and downside risk in my portfolio, so I could have a better chance of having a dignified retirement. In other words, I was seeking to avoid "sequence of returns risk". Sequence of returns risk is where you have a serious market decline in the years just before retirement or in early retirement, creating a heightened risk of running out of money in your old age, which would be bad.

My friend Atul Nautiyal, a Geophysicist in Calgary, told me about Harry Browne's Permanent Portfolio (HBPP), a portfolio configured to endure four conditions: recession, inflation, deflation... or growth. This portfolio consists of four things only, in equal parts:

1. U.S. stocks (25%)
2. 20 - 30 year U.S. Treasury bonds (25%)
3. Gold (25%)
4. Cash (25%)

When you backtest this asset allocation at sites like PortfolioVisualizer.com, it has amazingly smooth and consistent growth over a 45 year period, 1971 - 2016. There was hardly a bobble through the Tech Bubble and the Great Recession. Then, user "Tyler" at the HBPP online discussion forum, who is also on Twitter as @portfoliocharts, came up with a variation of the HBPP which he calls the "Golden Butterfly" (GB).

1. U.S. large-cap blend stocks (20%)
2. U.S. small-cap value stocks (20%)
3. 20 - 30 year U.S. Treasury bonds (20%)
4. Short-term U.S. Treasury bills / bonds (20%)
5. Gold (20%)

The GB is also low volatility, but has more growth than the HBPP. Now, I have since decided that the HBPP and GB are not allocations for me at this time, because I am seeking more growth during the current accumulation phase of my investing life. However, I think the Golden Butterfly could be a terrific post-retirement portfolio candidate. I need to hold that thought for the next ten years, especially if gold goes "on sale" between now and 2026. At any rate, Pandora's Box was opened, and I was off researching other ideas.

As I continued to search for portfolios, I ran into work by Dr. Mebane Faber (not to be confused with "Doctor Gloom Marc Faber"). Meb wrote a book titled, "The Ivy Portfolio", wherein he described a portfolio broadly similar to the endowments of Ivy League Universities like Harvard and Yale. His basic "Ivy 5" portfolio looks like this:

1. U.S. stocks (20%)
2. Foreign (non-U.S.) stocks (20%)
3. Real Estate (20%)
4. Aggregate bonds (20%)
5. Commodities (you could use Gold) (20%)

This allocation does well enough when back-tested to the early 1970s, but what really caught my attention was Faber's use of the 10-month moving average to move in and out of these assets as they trend up or trend down, just as we discussed in Chapter 1 on oil prices. This is called "Tactical Asset Allocation", or just Tactical. When you apply Tactical to the Ivy 5, you get stock market returns with bond market levels of risk, a nice result. This is also a good candidate for a post-retirement account, and I am testing it for that purpose now.

Finally, in late 2015, I read Gary Antonacci's book on "Dual Momentum" (DM) and was very captivated by it, and DM features prominently in how I invest today. Gary is a highly sought-after advisor and public speaker, but I was fortunate to meet him in person and we correspond by e-mail. He demonstrates a way to use momentum measures as a Tactical tool, to transition between US stocks, Foreign stocks, and Aggregate Bonds in a way that soundly beats being always fully invested in the stock market, over a full economic cycle. I got in touch with Gary, and he referred me to a couple of advisors who manage money using his proprietary E-GEM strategy, and I engaged one of them to handle one of my IRAs.

At present, our family retirement assets consist of:

1. Managed Tactical E-GEM (Antonacci)
2. Do-it-yourself Tactical Ivy5 (Faber)
3. Buy and hold stocks, real estate, and precious metals
4. Buy and hold diversified bond portfolio
5. Cash

I wish to emphasize that Tactical is not widely accepted as a mainstream investment strategy for the general public, it is considered a form of trading; therefore, it should only be utilized by a sophisticated and fully-informed investor.

There are signs the financial services industry is paying attention to us "finance geek hobbyists" playing in the corners, and the staid conservatism of this industry may be changing. I was encouraged to read the following statement from INVESCO from July 2015:

"In the past, alternative investments were the exclusive domain of institutional and high-net-worth investors," said Walter Davis, Alternatives Strategist at Invesco. "The Goodbye 60/40, Hello 50/30/20 campaign highlights the point that **different alternatives** have the potential to help investors achieve their timeless investment goals of building wealth, preserving wealth and/or generating enhanced current income and should be seen as core building blocks of mainstream portfolios."

"Different alternatives" is code for gold, commodities, real estate, tactical, managed futures, and options.

This journey from plain vanilla investor to tactical and buy-and-hold investor making use of stocks, bonds, and alternative investments took 19 months from start to finish. Losing my job was a big catalyst in speeding me along on this journey, because I realized that it was all "on me" - I would never again have the opportunity to have an employer who was going to take care of me with a generous defined-benefit pension.

I know I made some mistakes along the way. I got into some bad trades, and acquired some bruises but no lasting injuries. The great thing is, I found several good ideas and met some helpful and even famous people during my quest. I hope my personal history conveyed here speeds up and eases your own journey towards a more secure and self-determined future.

In summary, if you decide to use an advisor, you need to understand their compensation model, if they are acting as a fiduciary, their training and licenses, are they a real advisor, and do your investing styles match? If you answer those questions well, you probably have the basis for a good working relationship.

Appendix B - An Eclectic List of Resources

The following listings are unsolicited and uncompensated

Budgeting & Saving Money Websites

Dave Ramsey
www.daveramsey.com

Clark Howard
www.clark.com

Mint.com - phone app and desktop computer browser app

Investing and Asset Allocation Reading

Antonacci, Gary (2015), Dual Momentum Investing: An Innovative Strategy for Higher Returns with Lower Risk, New York, McGraw-Hill Education

Related blog: www.optimalmomentum.com

Faber, Mebane T. (2015), Global Asset Allocation: A Survey of the World's Top Investment Strategies, The Idea Farm L.P.

Faber, Mebane T., and Richardson, Eric W. (2009), The Ivy Portfolio: How to Invest Like the Top Endowments and Avoid Bear Markets, Hoboken, NJ: John Wiley & Sons, Inc.

>Related blog: mebfaber.com

Gray, Wesley R., Vogel, Jack R., and Foulke, David P. (2015), DIY Financial Advisor: A Simple Solution to Build and Protect Your Wealth, Hoboken, NJ: John Wiley & Sons, Inc.

Rowland, Craig, and Lawson, J.M. (2012), The Permanent Portfolio: Harry Browne's long-term investing strategy, Hoboken, NJ: John Wiley & Sons, Inc.

>Companion non-commercial discussion forum: www.gyroscopicinvesting.com

Schwab-Pomerantz, Carrie, and Cuthbertson, Joanne (2014), The Charles Schwab Guide to Finances After Fifty, New York: Crown Business

Free non-commercial web-based financial modeling and charting tools

PortfolioVisualizer.com

PortfolioCharts.com

www.StockCharts.com

Discount Brokerage Firms for traditional Do-It-Yourselfers

Charles Schwab and Co., Inc.
www.schwab.com

Fidelity Investments
www.fidelity.com

T.Rowe Price
www.troweprice.com

The Vanguard Group
www.vanguard.com

Robo-advisors for Do-It-Yourselfers who want to use automation and technology

www.alphaarchitect.com

www.betterment.com

www.cambriainvestments.com

intelligent.schwab.com

www.wealthfront.com

Fee-based Advisors for those who need Guidance

Ameriprise Financial
www.ameriprise.com
Joseph Silva, CPA
10375 Richmond Ave., Suite 1420
Houston, TX 77042-4124
Phone (713) 954-4940
joseph.l.silva@ampf.com

Edward Jones
www.edwardjones.com

Lance Jones, AAMS®
2815 West Lake Houston Parkway, Suite 108
Kingwood, TX 77339
(281) 361-0667
lance.jones@edwardjones.com

Shrier Associates
www.shrierassociates.com
Rick Shrier, CLU, CFC
619 Devenwood Way
Clinton, MA 01510
Phone (508) 898-9500
info@shrierassociates.com

Recommendations fron Clark Howard:

> National Association of Personal Financial Advisers
> NAPFA.org
>
> Garrett Planning Network
> GarrettPlanningNetwork.com

Insurance Providers

> Doug Roufa, CLU ChFC
> www.roufainsurance.com
> Phone (281) 277-0474
> roufains@ureach.com
>
> www.SelectQuote.com
>
> www.ZanderIns.com
>
> www.HealthCare.gov

ABOUT THE AUTHOR

Peter Wang MS PG MBA CRPC® began his Oil & Gas career in 1986 at Amoco Production Company (now BP). He progressed to Paradigm, Kelman Seismic Processing, Schlumberger, then back to Paradigm in 2015, where he is currently a Geophysical Technical Advisor. He earned an ScB in Geological Sciences from Brown University, and both an MS in Geophysics and an MBA from the University of Houston. In 2016, he earned the Chartered Retirement Planning Counselor^{SM} (CRPC®) designation. He is also a Texas Licensed Professional Geoscientist (PG). Peter welcomes comments and questions.

Contact information:

Facebook Group "Financial Survival for Oil Workers"
https://www.facebook.com/groups/OilGasWork/

Email: pwang01@gmail.com

Voicemail: (832) 582-0514